UNTANGLING COMMUNICATION

How Leaders Can Strengthen Communication,
Resolve Conflict,
and Build High-Performing Teams

Maria Garaitonandia

Copyright © 2025 Maria Garaitonandia

All rights reserved.

No part of this publication may be reproduced, stored in a retrieval system or transmitted in any form or by any means—electronic, mechanical, photocopying, recording, or otherwise —without prior written permission from the author.

The material in this book is intended for informational purposes only. While every effort has been made to ensure the accuracy of the content, the author assumes no responsibility for errors, omissions or different interpretations. This publication is not intended as a substitute for professional advice. Readers are encouraged to seek appropriate professional guidance for their specific circumstances.

Published by Global Bridges Publishing

www.globalbridgestraining.com

Interior Design and Cover Design by Rasel Khondokar

Library of Congress Control Number: 2025913179

ISBN (Paperback): 979-8-9988210-0-4

ISBN (ebook): 979-8-9988210-1-1

Printed in the United States of America

Dedication

To all the leaders navigating the mystery and tangle of communication. To those who wonder whether they're saying too much or too little, or if their words are landing the way they intend, balancing clarity with compassion.

To those striving to motivate while staying true to themselves as they guide their teams toward greater harmony and connection.

The fact that you care enough to untangle it speaks volumes about your commitment to creating something better. This book is for you.

Contents

Introduction: The Tangles That Trip Up Leaders 2

Chapter 1: The Real Cost of Getting Communication Wrong . 7
    Why We Keep Spinning in Circles 7
    The Toolbox Principle 10
    Summary: The Knots That Stall Success 18
    Untangling the Knots 19

Chapter 2: Conflict and Trust in Communication 22
    The Amygdala Challenge 22
    Empathy as a Bridge to Trust 28
    Vulnerability and Trust 34
    Summary: The Knots That Break Teams 40
    Untangling the Knots 40

Chapter 3: Feedback in Communication 43
    Trauma-Free Feedback 43
    Redefining Feedback 44
    The Cost of Zero Feedback 45
    Recognition that Resonates 46
    The CARE Model for Recognition Feedback 50
    The FRAME Model for Corrective Feedback 54
    Receiving Feedback 71
    Summary: The Knots that Trigger Defensiveness 75
    Untangling the Knots 76

Chapter 4: Cross-Cultural Communication 79
Lessons from a Third Culture Kid 79
Navigating Corporate Culture 86
Our Cultural Lens 88
Communicating in a Cross-Cultural Environment 94
Low-Context Communication 101
High-Context Communication 104
Summary: The Knots of that Distort Meaning 107
Untangling the Knots 108

Chapter 5: Generations, Technology, and Communication 111
The Death of the Phone Call 111
Fostering a Culture of Connection 117
Connection and Social Media 120
Building Rapport in a Digital Age 124
Hardwired for Connection 129
L.E.A.D. for Connection 132
Summary: The Knots that Block Connection 138
Untangling the Knots: 138

Chapter 6: Untangling Communication 141
The Underlying Message 141
The Communication Process 144
Everyday CLEAR Communication 146

Conclusion: The Thread that Ties It All Together 155

Appendix A: Is Your Team Tied Up in Knots?
A Self-Diagnosis Tool 160

v

Appendix B: New Team Alignment Blueprint:
   Setting the Stage for Success 164

Appendix C: Cultural Snapshots: High-Context vs.
   Low-Context Communication 166

Appendix D: Ice-Breaking Questions for Virtual Teams 171

References by Chapter 173

The single biggest problem in communication is the illusion that it has taken place.

—George Bernard Shaw

INTRODUCTION

The Tangles That Trip Up Leaders

"You need to apply baby powder when you speak to people here!"

My father, an executive for a global company, was transferred to different countries during my childhood and adolescence, and I remember his assignment in Mexico taking a particularly hard toll on him. His blunt, straightforward Cuban style didn't sit very well in a culture that valued courtesy and face-saving.

He complained that he didn't understand why his people were so difficult, why the locals were so sensitive, why they couldn't just do this or that. Not knowing how to relate to the people that surrounded him or pick up on the unspoken rules was a source of very real stress for him. What should have been a successful expatriate assignment as Financial Director weighed heavily on him, and we all felt it at home.

Seeing him struggle may have been one of the reasons I became interested in the mysteries of human communication. I needed to figure out what he hadn't. When I spoke to him about the experience years later, he recognized how ill-prepared he was and how little his and other organizations did to prepare their leaders to be successful in the human interaction aspect of the job. When thrust into the deep end of a new cultural environment or other leadership roles, they quickly learned it was sink or swim.

My dad was transferred every few years, so I was what they call a Third Culture Kid,[1] having spent a great deal of my formative years outside that of our home culture. As we moved between countries and cultures, I learned how gestures, tone, and even silence carried meaning. I often found myself in the role of interpreter, sensing the unspoken dynamics in a room. I could tell, for example, if a certain expression used by someone, even in the same language, could have a negative impact on someone else.

This experience, and many others like it, planted a seed. Over time, I realized that the ability to untangle these interactions and uncover the true intentions behind words and actions formed a lifeline for building trust and encouraging collaboration in teams. It extended beyond the intercultural, though. Interpreting cultural nuances, I came to understand, required the same skillset needed in other communication scenarios.

How does this connect with leadership? Well, think about it. Most leaders endure constant pressure to get things done; meet deadlines, drive results, and keep teams aligned. But often, what derails progress isn't the technical challenges as much as the human ones. That was precisely what made it hard for my dad to align with his team. He just didn't get them, and they didn't get him—and that disconnect made it harder to reach their goals.

That struggle stuck with me. And for the past couple of decades, I've helped my clients navigate these complexities, get to the heart of their message, and lead with confidence. Ultimately, I realized that communication was at the heart of it all. But how we perceive it

---

[1] Pollock, David C., Ruth E. Van Reken, and Michael V. Pollock. *Third Culture Kids: Growing Up Among Worlds.* 3rd ed. Boston: Nicholas Brealey Publishing, 2017.

makes a huge difference in how we approach it. Is it a big, messy knot full of chaos or a smooth string that ties things together?

Any time I've asked what makes a good leader, "effective communicator" is high on the list. But what does that look like? How do leaders deal with the challenges we face today? If you're a leader, do any of these challenges sound familiar?

- Is conflict ignored or escalated, making it harder for stakeholders to align and move forward?
- Do projects stall because of unclear communication or lack of meaningful feedback?
- Are there cross-cultural issues in your global teams that cause friction or misunderstandings?
- Are there generational disconnects that cause confusion or frustration among team members?
- Despite all the tools designed to connect us, are meaningful interactions with stakeholders still difficult to establish?

If these situations sound familiar, welcome to the club. Communication challenges are in the forefront of so many leadership struggles, and they don't come with an easy playbook. One study by The Economist Intelligence Unit found that poor communication contributes to increased stress (52 percent of employees), failure to complete projects (44 percent), and low morale (31 percent)[2].

---

[2] The Economist Intelligence Unit, *Communication Barriers in the Modern Workplace* (The Economist Group, 2018).

When communication breaks down, consequences ripple through an organization. Progress stalls, relationships are strained, and teams feel frustrated and disconnected, sometimes forcing leaders to play referee and resolve tensions without a clear guide to navigate them.

The goal of this book is to give you the tools to untangle these knots and weave threads that strengthen your team. A key element of this transformation lies in the ability to navigate the nuances of human connection and read between the lines, even in the most challenging moments.

In the twenty-five years I've been coaching, teaching, and training, I've heard the same communication challenges surface again and again. So, I have determined to make it my life's work to help people navigate through the labyrinth of confusion and build clarity, respect and goodwill into their messages. To me it's like unraveling a big knot—frustrating at first but incredibly satisfying when you finally see the string smoothed, moving from chaos to harmony.

This book tackles the messy reality of team communication. You'll learn practical strategies to untangle communication misunderstandings, build trust and create alignment within your team. From handling conflict to closing gaps between cultures or generations, I'll walk you through proven approaches that work. Each chapter includes examples and techniques you can try right away. Plus, there are assessment tools in the back to help you.

Leadership is a journey, and communication is the map. Time to chart your course.

Communication is not about speaking what we think.
Communication is about ensuring others hear what we mean.

— **Simon Sinek**

CHAPTER 1

The Real Cost of Getting Communication Wrong

---•||•---

Why We Keep Spinning in Circles

I'd been stuck on the last step of a fiscal process in an international client's portal and couldn't move forward. I was instructed by my stakeholder to contact Daniel, the support guy.

I wrote to Daniel, explaining my problem and then moved on to something else. A day and a half later, Daniel responded, though his email didn't answer my question. I sighed and elaborated, giving more context, sharing screenshots with colored arrows in my attempt at clarification, and finally suggested a phone call. More days passed; Daniel ignored my request but sent another cryptic message with a document attached containing instructions like the one I had already been using.

At this point I wanted to scream. I confess to passing all kinds of harsh judgments in my head. What was wrong with this guy? Was he ignoring me on purpose? Did his email mean that he couldn't care less about what I did? Perhaps he was just implying that I was dumb! My criticisms continued. Was he incompetent or just indifferent? Or both?

Since his email signature lacked a phone number (which increased my annoyance tenfold), my next email had to convince him to agree to talk to me. I took a deep breath and started writing, sure to establish what was in it for him, so instead of going back and forth, could we please just have a ten-minute call?

He finally agreed to a video call, and we solved the problem in ten minutes. Previously, I had probably wasted about two hours developing emails over a three-week period. How exhausting. Does this type of experience sound familiar?

What happened here isn't rare. In fact, a 2023 Grammarly and Harris Poll[3] found that US companies lose over $12,500 per employee per year due to communication breakdowns, a staggering cost, especially when so many of those breakdowns could be avoided with a five-minute conversation. Daniel and I probably contributed more than our fair share of that statistic with our inefficient communication.

Now, if I wanted to quantify that, I could analyze the weeks that it took to solve the problem, the delay in the project deployment and return on investment for my client, plus the time I put into each email, complete with references and screenshots. Even if I had used AI to write my emails, I would have had to give it the right prompts and information. No matter how we look at it, all the alternatives would require much more time and effort than a real-time exchange.

As a consultant who specializes in communications-related issues, I've encountered many clients struggling with communication breakdowns in their teams, hindering their processes and negatively impacting results. Looking deeper, however, I came to note a common thread. The Harris poll report stated that people are

---

3 Grammarly Business and The Harris Poll, *2023 State of Business Communication* (Grammarly, Inc., 2023).

relying more than ever on written and asynchronous communication such as emails, chats, and document collaboration platforms, while reducing verbal real-time communication found in face-to-face, video, or phone meetings.

The latest Harris report confirms that more than half of our work week is consumed by written communication,[4] and although generative AI has helped us improve in certain areas, we must optimize our usage of these tools, not just use more of them. Many companies report a gap between what is out there and how people are using this new technology.

This trend toward reliance on more written communication remains on the rise, yet it's not producing better results. Just think about it: It takes longer to communicate in written form than in verbal, especially considering, according to that study, that many people fret about using the right words and tone in their missives. And probably for good reasons. Another study published in *Organization Management Journal* found that perceived rudeness in an email creates a more negative result than in a face-to-face interaction.[5] It makes sense, since we don't have the benefit of the tone and non-verbal context and thus we may be quicker to interpret a snub in a written message.

Let's unpack that. More and more, people are talking less and less to each other and opting for written forms of communication, despite tons of technological tools that permit us to be virtually

---

[4] Grammarly and The Harris Poll, *2024 State of Business Communication* (Grammarly Inc., 2024).

[5] Kimberly, McCarthy, Jone L. Pearce, John Morton, and Sarah Lyon. "Do You Pass It On? The Effect of Perceived Incivility on Task Performance and the Performance Evaluations of Others." *Organization Management Journal (2020).*

present at the touch of a button. Cell phones are rarely used as phones anymore and landlines are practically extinct. Societal protocol has deemed spontaneous calling undesirable and invasive. It's not so commonplace these days for colleagues to just hit the call button on their internal text platforms. The rules now dictate that we must write first and request permission to verbally engage.

Engaging without permission is usually reserved for emergencies or preluded by an apologetic explanation. Most times, an unexpected call will go unanswered, perceived as presumptuous and intrusive. Instead, people will formally request an audience and patiently wait for it to be granted. If not, communication gets stalled, and stuff doesn't get done. Hence, the mega money wasted in lost productivity and inefficiency.

That means that regardless of all our software and devices, we remain stuck in a rut when it comes to communication. As in other areas of life, we may have many options at our disposal but may be stuck on just one way of doing things, missing an opportunity to be more effective (and efficient). We'll take a look at the impact of technology and generational habits in more detail later on, but it's important to be flexible in our use of communication tools according to the objective.

The Toolbox Principle

A client once told me that his team had doubled in size, but after a full year, none of the new members knew anyone else personally since all work was done remotely, resulting in a noticeable lack of connection, trust, and collaboration overall. Upon developing an in-person teambuilding workshop for his team, I was surprised to hear various conversations go something like this:

"Oh, you're Adela? I'm Christian. We've been working together on project 'X'." Adela would then smile warmly, delighted to put a face to a name. That exchange and others left me thinking: *Okay, these two have been working together remotely for months and yet didn't know what the other one looked like? No wonder the team is disconnected if members perceive each other as faceless strangers and abstract concepts more than colleagues!* Most didn't even have a photo in their internal profile.

Now before you say, "Screen fatigue," I get it, the pandemic forced us into a virtual world, and yes, in many cases, this has become the new way of doing things, but it's been a while, so that excuse has gotten old and now we need to make sure the remedy isn't worse than the malady. The screen is now part of our life, whether we like it or not.

Plenty of research exists on the topic, with as many differing opinions as there are preferences, but the pros offer some strong arguments that align with productivity and clear communication. Among fascinating statistics and data, researchers have determined that simply seeing our colleague or stakeholder helps us build trust, gives us more exposure to people, holds us accountable, decreases the probability of misinterpretation, keeps us focused, fosters team cohesion, and encourages reciprocity.[6] Pretty strong case for the visual, if you ask me.

---

[6] Steve Hughes, "Top 10 Reasons to Keep Your Camera on in Virtual Meetings," *LinkedIn*, April 18, 2022.

I know from my past experiences conducting virtual training or coaching sessions that the instant my participants turn their webcams on, I feel a shift in my sense of connection. A rush of dopamine hits me when they reveal their faces for the first time after hearing their voices initially. This visual contact creates connection, making those I interact with seem more relatable; a new sense of solidarity and intimacy emerges.

Before conducting my session, I explain that emulating an in-person experience as much as possible, with everyone turning on their webcams, will provide the richest experience. This helps set expectations and facilitates buy-in. Most comply, although a few holdouts offering all kinds of excuses (bad internet, bad hair day, driving, eating, unresponsive webcam, under the weather day, etc.) may show up. After repeating why visual connection is so important and requesting that they do their utmost to correct the situation, I usually get most participants on their webcams at some point.

Of course, those who oppose the process may have valid concerns, such as privacy or a desire to avoid feeling self-conscious about looking presentable.[7] The latter isn't a great excuse anymore, since current technology offers better background and blurring capabilities for privacy as well as enhancing filters on most meeting platforms. I confess, I love that applying make-up has become optional, having discovered enhancing filters with nice lipstick shades, eyelashes and skin smoothers on most communication software programs. I tell my participants that hair-combing is also

---

[7] Gleb Tsipursky, "Cameras on or off? How to Settle the Debate on Video Calls for Good." *Fast Company* June 20, 2023.

optional, and let's be honest, most of us wear pajama bottoms and slippers anyway.

For me, self-view can be distracting. I find myself focusing on being self-critical of my face rather than the conversation. Turning self-view off allows me to be more present and natural, as I would be in an in-person session with no mirror reflecting my every move.

That said, while not every meeting requires cameras on, it's not a great idea to be a stranger to your teammates. How to strike the right balance between ensuring team members their privacy when required while bolstering teamwork and collaboration through visual contact? It's important to choose the right tool from the toolbox.

Let's use the analogy of a hammer as the tool. A hammer may be very practical for attaching a nail to the wall, but trying to use it to attach a screw or cut a piece of wood is probably not the best idea.

Written communication can sometimes act as a hammer, which may simply be too blunt for the task of understanding certain concepts or building rapport. Using a hammer on the screw can damage it, in the same way a relationship may get strained due to overdone written communication.

So why would written communication be too blunt of an instrument in some cases?

It lacks warmth and tone: There's no tone or body language, and very little subtext used to build connection. We can hammer away at a flat surface or piece of wood, but we risk warping or cracking it if we overdo it. I know some people use emojis (even in business communications), but little cartoonish faces can't substitute for human interaction.

It limits response: It's much slower and harder to have immediate clarification or adjustment based on the receiver's reaction. It's like hammering away at a nail without checking to see whether it's going in straight.

It can come across as harsh: The formality of writing can sometimes make requests sound more forceful or demanding than intended, just like constant hammering can feel aggressive. It can also convey the underlying message that the other party is a secondary priority or an afterthought.

All this should help drive home the fact that just because we may feel more comfortable with one type of communication doesn't mean it's the right one to use every time. AI may help us craft beautiful messages, but they still take time to request, edit and (hopefully) get answered. The same limitations exist.

When it came to Daniel, there were two options: continue using the hammer relentlessly with no results on the horizon, or switch tools. I realized we needed a screwdriver, not a hammer. So, with tact, I decided to stop talking about the problem and start talking about our interaction. I began with the obvious fact that this was taking us nowhere and we really needed to talk. Although I was thoroughly frustrated, I started by focusing on him and indicating that I didn't want to waste more of *his* time than necessary (even though I was more concerned with my own) and to please grant me a few minutes to solve this quickly. Presenting the win-win scenario was key in persuading him.

> I decided to stop talking about the problem and start talking about our interaction.

But why did it take so long to have that ten-minute conversation? It's understandable that we're doing more and more every day, but here's where we need to quantify the results we obtain through faulty processes.

When it comes to deciding whether to engage in written or verbal communication, it can be easy to default to our preferred mode. There's a feeling that once we send that message, we're done and off the hook, until we realize that nothing is getting done or we're running out of time. Before we get to that point, we can ask ourselves:

- Is this something I can resolve more quickly or efficiently with a conversation?
- What's preventing me from just resolving this in real time?
- Can this wait? If so, how long?
- How much time have I spent already and what results have I seen so far?

If we find ourselves going back and forth, investing more time in written communication than we would on a call, perhaps it's time to rethink our communication strategy. Choosing the right channel is just one element to consider when striving to improve team communication. In Appendix A, you'll find a self-diagnosis tool that may help you as a leader to determine what areas you might want to focus on.

There's a moment for a hammer and a moment for a screwdriver. When choosing our tools, we should be well versed in the use of each. A one-size-fits-all approach won't work, even if it feels more comfortable to just send off an email and be done with it.

Combining tools with a situational approach provides flexibility to adapt to different situations.

Instead of running around in circles and running out of energy, we can imagine filling our tank with **GAS**. It can help to think about the **Goal**, **Audience**, and **Situation** before picking our communication method. It may be helpful to ask ourselves:

Goal: What do I need to accomplish with this communication?

- **Clarity and precision**: When it comes to outlining details, instructions, or a large quantity of information, written communication may work well initially if it's clear and can be easily referred to. However, further verbal clarification or follow-up may be necessary to move ahead or cement commitment, as was in my case with Daniel. The more written communication involved, the higher the chance of things getting lost in the shuffle.

- **Building Rapport and Connection**: Real-time interaction builds trust in a way emails and messages never could. A voice or shared laugh strengthens relationships and humanizes the conversation. Without it, we're often left communicating with a concept rather than a person.

- **Quick Updates or Simple Questions**: Informal channels such as instant messaging or short emails are probably good in these instances. No need for a meeting if a two-sentence response will do the trick.

- **Brainstorming and Collaboration**: If we're sharing ideas and need active participation, those visual cues help participants see how some ideas land, as it gives real-time feedback.

Audience: Who am I communicating with?

- **Unknown Stakeholders**: First impressions matter. A visible, welcoming presence fosters trust and makes interactions more personal. That said, an initial or follow up email adds a level of professionalism and documentation.
- **Close Colleagues**: Depending on your relationship, expectations and context, a quick interoffice chat or a call may be helpful.
- **Larger Groups:** In cases in which people are mostly listening and not actively participating, video conferencing, coupled with a follow-up email, ensures clarity and can even include reference materials.

Situation: What is happening, and how does that affect message's reception?

- **Sensitive situations**: Clarity and context can be gauged far more accurately through facial expressions and body language. A face-to-face or verbal conversation (in person or via video) helps to ensure tone and nuance aren't lost.
- **Urgency**: If you need an immediate response, a phone call or instant message usually gets faster results than email.
- **Time-sensitivity**: For important tasks, we can use two forms of communication. For example, a follow-up email after a call to ensure things move forward smoothly. Status updates that aren't urgent can be managed by what some call an audio "walking meeting,"[8] (aka phone call).

---

[8] Allison S. Gabriel, Daron Robertson, and Kristen Shockley. "Research: Cameras On or Off?" *Harvard Business Review*, October 26, 2021.

Leaders drive the culture in their teams and organizations, setting the tone and determining the behavior that will be recognized or discouraged. I can't count the times I've had leaders mention difficulty creating cohesion in their group and then finding out that all their meetings are conducted virtually with cameras off.

Embracing something as simple as turning webcams on occasionally to create a sense of camaraderie and accountability can make a tangible difference. There's no need to cling to habits that stall communication and strain relationships.

Ultimately, neglecting human connection comes at a significant cost in time, effort, and resources. While written communication serves a purpose, it can't replace the power of verbal real-time interaction. Leaders who embrace the "toolbox principle" and prioritize real-time connection, including using webcams strategically, can foster engagement and alignment, as well as a more productive work environment.

Just as a hammer isn't great for tightening screws, no single communication method works for every situation. The GAS model (think of filling your tank, not the other kind) can help us be well versed when it comes to the use of different tools, so we can be intentional about choosing which one best fits the purpose. When we match the method to the moment, we build momentum.

Summary: The Knots That Stall Success

In addition to causing headaches, miscommunication is a costly drain on businesses. Consider my situation with Daniel, struggling over emails for weeks on a simple issue. This is common in workplaces and one reason U.S. companies lose so much money annually because of poor communication.

Part of the problem often lies in relying too much on written communication for tasks better suited to real-time conversations or avoiding webcams altogether. Emails and messages may seem efficient, but they can often create confusion and delay decisions.

When it comes to video calls, many avoid turning their cameras on, thinking it's not an important factor. But non-verbal cues, such as facial expressions and body language are essential for clear communication. Without them, misunderstandings grow, and teams feel more disconnected.

Untangling the Knots

Before defaulting to another email or switching off the camera in a virtual meeting consider using the "toolbox principle" and asking yourself:

- Could a call or video chat clear things up more quickly?
- Is written communication causing delays or misunderstandings?
- Is the message getting lost without face-to-face interaction?

Use the **GAS** principle to guide your choice:

- **Goal** — What's your intended outcome?
- **Audience** — Who are you communicating with, and what's their style?
- **Situation** — What's the urgency or complexity of the matter?

In short, be strategic. Effective communication doesn't hinge on using one method, but rather on selecting the right one.

As we move forward, the question we must ask ourselves is: How do we respond when communication breaks down? Even with the best intentions, things can get tense as emotions run high. Next, we'll dive into what happens when we hit those rough tangles, and how we can face conflict without letting it pull us apart.

Between stimulus and response, there is a space. In that space is our power to choose our response. In our response lies our growth and our freedom

— Viktor E. Frankl

CHAPTER 2

Conflict and Trust in Communication

The Amygdala Challenge

I'm not proud of this, but here goes. Years ago, I was driving in Mexico City and needed to merge onto a highway. An SUV came up behind me and cut me off on the ramp. I had to break hard to avoid it.

I was startled but also infuriated by this driver's selfish imprudence and his utter disdain for my safety. I reacted and simply sped up, passed him, got in his lane and broke hard. I was satisfied I had gotten revenge. The only problem was it didn't end there. He sped up, cut me off a second time, and then came to a complete stop in the right-hand lane on the highway.

My adrenaline was pumping so hard. My anger compounded with fear. I was in full fight mode and grateful for my black belt in karate because it seemed like things were about to get real very quickly. The man got out of his car, and I got out of mine. I wasn't quite sure what I thought would happen. We made eye contact. In seconds, I became aware of so many things.

As he walked toward me, I saw clearly that he wanted to fight, but then he saw me. I noticed his look of disappointment. In his face I could see my own bitterness reflected back at me. What a sobering moment. Suddenly, the urgency of the situation seemed to melt away. The story I had concocted in my head about this selfish jerk who wanted to harm me didn't seem so absolute anymore.

He sighed and spoke. "*Señora*, you cut in front of me!" The courtesy title sounded strange, considering what had happened a few moments ago. I found myself following suit. "Yes, *señor*, I just wanted you to see how it felt."

He shook his head and walked away. And just like that, our road rage incident was over. I'm ashamed to tell this story, but the truth is, it was an indelible learning experience. I was lucky that this situation didn't result in a tragedy. A friend whom I recounted this story to said that the universe was trying to teach me something and this guy was a messenger. I was going through a difficult time in my life, which probably made me more susceptible to the small trigger that escalated in seconds. I'll bet he was too.

I know now that I was reacting to everything I had been carrying, not just to the driver. That incident made clear how easily emotions can hijack our better judgement and how fast our brains can push us into action before we even know what we're doing.

The thing is it *could* have ended in tragedy. Afterward, I asked myself, *What was I thinking? How could I, a rational person, get worked up into such a frenzy that I put myself in real danger?* But I wasn't thinking. We feel first, and it takes a while for the rational mind to catch up with our emotions, allowing for a thoughtful response during stressful situations. This part is key, and the reason we hear the age-old adage, "Count to ten," before reacting.

This overwhelming emotional response, or amygdala hijack[9], is what Daniel Goleman describes in his book *Emotional Intelligence*, a response during which the brain reacts to something it sees as a threat before logic has a chance to catch up. It typically manifests with:

An emotional surge: The amygdala sends out strong emotional signals that can overpower the rational thinking part of the brain, the neocortex.

Impulse over reason: The ability to think logically may be momentarily sidelined, leading to impulsive actions based on raw emotion.

Physical reactions: We may experience a racing heartbeat, flushed face, or tense muscles as the body prepares to "fight" the perceived threat.

In the context of road rage, the amygdala hijack explains why my minor incident escalated into such a heated exchange. I was already carrying an emotional burden when my brain perceived the other driver's actions as a personal attack, triggering an immediate and intense emotional reaction before I had the chance to think it through.

Resisting the urge to react to triggering emotions is easier said than done. It takes a high level of self-awareness to catch yourself in the moment, before the emotion takes control. Sadly, I failed that challenge on that fateful morning in Mexico City. That lack of

---

[9] Daniel Goleman, *Emotional Intelligence: Why It Can Matter More Than IQ*, 2nd ed, (New York: Bantam Books, 1995), 27-45.

awareness cascaded into a lack of self-control, and I spiraled into reaction without for a moment considering the other person.

Empathy is the cornerstone of emotional intelligence, and while I was sure that this man was simply an imprudent selfish jerk, I didn't know his story. I had no idea what he was going through, if he was distracted, distraught or depressed. I just jumped to conclusions and went with my narrative and gut reaction.

The Amygdala Hijack in Modern Life

But road rage isn't the only example of when an amygdala hijack can get the best of us. Things can accumulate and then blow up when we least expect it, especially considering other factors that may be present. The amygdala is one of the brain's most primitive structures, developed to ensure our ancestors' survival by reacting quickly to threats.

When our brain perceives danger, whether it's a physical threat such as encountering a predator or an emotional one, in the form of, say feeling disrespected on the road, the amygdala floods our system with signals that release adrenaline and cortisol. These hormones prepare the body for "fight, flight, or freeze," all necessary reaction in life-threatening situations.

However, the issue in modern life is that our amygdala hasn't adapted to distinguish between true physical threats and emotional or social ones. It reacts to both in the same way. The reason this happens is that the amygdala processes sensory information faster than the prefrontal cortex, the rational, decision-making part of the brain.

As Joseph LeDoux explains in *The Emotional Brain*, the amygdala operates on a "low road" of emotional processing, designed to react quickly to danger without waiting for the slower, more rational processing of the "high road" through the neocortex[10]. This was beneficial when early humans needed to dodge a predator, but in the context of modern life, it can be ineffective, causing us to respond to emotional stress, like an inconsiderate driver, as if it were a physical threat.

LeDoux also points out that the amygdala is involved in emotional memory, meaning it stores and recalls past experiences of fear and anger. In my case, I was already going through personal challenges, and the emotional burden I carried likely made me more susceptible to feeling attacked by the driver's behavior. The amygdala, sensing a threat, didn't stop to differentiate between my emotional state and the reality of the situation—it just reacted. This is why, as Goleman stresses, emotional intelligence is crucial in helping us manage these instinctive reactions.

Even in a work environment we may get carried away with negative emotions if we perceive a threat. It may not be a physical threat, but instead one to our sense of self-worth, which causes us to escalate the conflict, making it more difficult to find a positive solution and damaging the relationship. But avoiding conflict isn't the solution, since the more we avoid it or let it simmer, the harder it is to resolve and the less inclined we are to find a mutually beneficial solution since the narrative in our heads tends to get more complicated as we second-guess the other person's intentions.

---

[10] Joseph, LeDoux, *The Emotional Brain: The Mysterious Underpinnings of Emotional Life*, (New York: Simon & Schuster, 1996).

As Goleman mentions in his book, the cornerstone of emotional intelligence is empathy. If we can change the story in our heads by changing the main character to be the other person, we're on the road to understanding. It's a really hard thing to do sometimes, but once we do it, it changes everything.

When working with groups in some of my programs, I have them dissect a recent conflict. Once we get to the analysis of probable causes for the other person's behavior, I see my participants shift and soften as they adjust their perspective.

When I ask them "What could the other person have been thinking or feeling?" they pause and grow a bit quiet, since many times they had never even thought about it. The narrative in their minds dealt only with how they were affected by the exchange, not how the other person was affected. Their attributions were what mattered, not any other possible explanations.

I remember a passage I read from Steven R. Covey's book *The 7 Habits of Highly Effective People* which affected me. He shared a story about a man on the subway whose children were misbehaving. Other passengers were getting irritated, and when Covey asked the man if he could control his children, the man, who seemed to be in a deep daze, explained that they were just coming from the hospital where his wife, their mother had died[11].

Upon hearing that, Covey felt a sudden emotional shift from irritation and impatience to a deep sense of compassion. As the reader, I felt the same. Everything else suddenly becomes trivial in the face of human suffering. This lesson highlights the power of

---

[11] Stephen R Covey, *The 7 Habits of Highly Effective People: Powerful Lessons in Personal Change,* (New York: Simon & Schuster, 1989).

shifting one's perspective in seeking to understand before reacting or passing judgments. It's like a blindfold coming off.

Do we ever really know what's going on with those around us? Are they carrying emotional burdens due to grief, heartbreak, illness or financial stress? We know we carry them, so why not give others the benefit of the doubt? By pausing to consider what the other person may be going through or what might be driving their behavior, we create space for empathy. This simple shift in perspective can change everything in how we manage conflict. It can strengthen our relationships and open the door to more positive and productive interactions.

Empathy as a Bridge to Trust
Reframing Conflict

A learning and development program manager told me about a situation in which an internal stakeholder requested a training program for his people. After the program was completed, the stakeholder wanted an extensive analysis of the results with specific elements measured. The program manager responded that his department didn't do that, but if the stakeholder wanted those reports, they could bill him for the hours, or he could hire a third party to do the work.

The stakeholder responded with a series of angry emails, escalating the situation to the program manager's own manager. Shocked and offended at the apparent aggression, the program manager's first thought was that this stakeholder was being difficult, petty, and unreasonable. He felt blindsided by the escalation and wrestled with the urge to lash back and defend himself.

Fortunately, though, he was able to stop, delay his response and take a good, honest look at his own role in the conflict. "I realized that instead of just placing up a barrier and washing my hands of it, I could have shown more interest in what he needed and why, and looked for solutions," he told me.

In that moment, making his stakeholder the main character of the narrative was the first step toward empathy and emotional intelligence. By exerting self-awareness and self-control, he reflected on what the stakeholder might have been feeling and recognized how his own response had contributed to the situation. He decided to mend the relationship, starting with an apology.

He then explained that, given limited resources, his department couldn't provide the requested service right now but that he was discussing the possibility of adding it in the future with his line manager. He also suggested they find a resource from the stakeholder's area to help with the data gathering in the meantime. The stakeholder's attitude softened, and they found a solution together, salvaging the relationship.

In a professional setting, the amygdala hijack can happen when we perceive a threat to our sense of competence, authority or self-worth. As communication expert Sam Horn says in *Talking on Eggshells*, "As soon as we have contempt, we have no compassion…it is the end of compassion, and it will lead to conflicts."

Just like my brain interpreted the other driver's actions as a threat to my safety, the program manager's brain likely perceived the stakeholder's demands as an attack on his professional competence. This triggers the same fight-or-flight response, but instead of slamming on the brakes or speeding up, we respond with sharp emails, defensive comments or passive-aggressive behavior.

Luckily, the program manager didn't go that route. He realized that the stakeholder's anger wasn't personal; it was likely driven by frustration over unmet expectations. Once he shifted his mindset from defensiveness to honest concern about the stakeholder's needs, he was able to address those needs, defuse the situation, and find a solution.

In both the workplace and everyday life, our ability to pause, reflect and shift from emotional reactivity to understanding is what separates constructive conflict from damaging escalation. Empathy can serve as the antidote to the amygdala hijack and allow us to move beyond the automatic responses that once served our survival but now often sabotage our relationships.

Changing the Narrative

On one occasion, a partner client hired me along with other trainers, to deliver content for a large client. "Jack" asked me to customize the program and deliver it in Spanish in Argentina and Mexico. I agreed, but wanted to negotiate a higher rate. He admitted he hadn't negotiated the customization with the client, so I suggested lowering his cut to compensate me for the extra work. I thought I argued my case brilliantly and assured him that the learning curve would be worth it. I added that he could re-negotiate with his client once they were satisfied with the first round.

After a few days of silence, I assumed he'd agreed and began making travel arrangements. When I finally heard from Jack, a week and a half later, he sent a long email explaining why he couldn't accommodate my rate. I was livid—not so much by the response itself, but over how long it took him to say no. I was tempted to tell him to find another Spanish-speaking trainer on short notice.

This time, however, I didn't let my amygdala get the best of me. My initial thought was that he was acting in bad faith, trying to pressure me into doing the session after I had already made travel arrangements. But then I changed the narrative. I decided to walk my own talk. I made Jack the main character and I thought about him. He wasn't a natural communicator; actually, he was a bit awkward. Could it be that he had taken this long because he didn't know how to say no? Or that he needed time to put his thoughts in order and try to break it to me gently and was overwhelmed by the thought?

I decided to give him the benefit of the doubt. When I wrote back, I told him I understood his position and that I would do the program, but perhaps next time he could negotiate for more with the client. Then in another paragraph, I told him I wanted to let him know that his delay in answering had left me feeling confused and disappointed, and I assumed it was because he was reluctant to give me the bad news. It would help in the future if he could respond quicker, since it made me feel very low on his list of priorities. I told him I was being honest since I wanted our professional relationship to thrive.

What happened next really surprised me. He answered me right away and apologized profusely, telling me that making me feel dismissed was the last thing he had intended, and lo and behold, agreed to the higher rate. He said he realized that our relationship was more important than the percentage of the revenue, and he didn't want me to walk away from our collaboration with a bad taste in my mouth. Wow.

Facing Relationship Issues Head-On

Jack's change in attitude confirmed how powerful it is to shift a conversation from a purely transactional tone to a relationship-centered one. Once I was open and honest, interpreting his actions in a positive light, he was able to see things differently. Putting aside the task at hand and addressing the relationship itself made a difference.

Many of my clients shy away from addressing relationship issues and try to sweep messy things under the rug and then wonder why some of their business partnerships falter. Talking about emotional topics in the workplace can seem awkward, but we're not merely human resources; we're people, and we shouldn't pretend otherwise. If we let the dust under the rug accumulate, eventually we will continuously trip and fall.

We don't need to reveal our deepest, darkest secrets, but being open enough to acknowledge the impact of others' behaviors makes us more relatable and invites reciprocity. After all, when someone confides in us, we value that connection, and it strengthens our bond.

So, what to do when a colleague or stakeholder has angered or offended us? We should resist the urge to avoid them, retaliate or escalate to a third party. Instead, we should go to them directly. This can be uncomfortable, but it can lead to surprisingly positive results, as it did with Jack, by strengthening relationships and boosting trust.

Our mindset in this first step is crucial. Even if we're feeling frustrated or hurt, this is where empathy is vital. While our instinct may be self-protection, we can take a moment to think about the situation from their perspective. Could something else be going on? What might explain their behavior?

When I stopped to consider that Jack was probably delaying the task of giving me the bad news because he may have felt overwhelmed, it was a little easier to forgive his tardiness in responding. He may have been considering my feelings in choosing his words carefully, even though his efforts backfired. This small change in perspective made it easier for me to approach him.

Here is a Conflict Conversation Cheat Sheet to help you prepare and stay focused under pressure.

https://globalbridgestraining.com/download-untangling-conflict-cheat-sheet/

Turning Conflict into Connection

I believe that most people are good and try their best, so there is no reason to assume the worst. The key to taking the next step is being brave and vulnerable at the same time. Sometimes we're too

> Most people are good and try their best, so there is no reason to assume the worst.

proud to admit that someone else has the power to affect us. Why do you think it's such a common reaction for people to answer angrily, "I'm not angry!" when asked if they are? It's an instinct to deny vulnerability, but admitting it, while handling the situation with control and grace, makes us stronger and more trustworthy.

The complete change in Jack's attitude told me how that change in perspective made a difference. He didn't know how his behavior affected me until I told him, and once I opened that door for him to see, he was able to understand me. That changed things. This is the shift that I encourage my clients to take.

Empathy, like any skill, becomes stronger the more we practice it. In the workplace, this means choosing to see the other side, even when it feels easier to defend ours. By stepping into someone else's shoes, we give ourselves a chance to respond thoughtfully rather than react impulsively. Ultimately, empathy promotes trust, which makes collaboration possible.

Vulnerability and Trust

When my kids were little, we often took them to a sports club where they'd play with other kids at the pool, while the mothers sat around and socialized. We'd take turns talking about our family dynamics, sharing frustrations with our kids and spouses, and laughing as we poked fun at ourselves. All except one— "Leah". Leah just smiled and laughed but never joined in. When she did speak, she was evasive, hinting that everything was "just peachy" in her household. Uh huh!

I get it. Maybe she didn't feel comfortable sharing. But her reluctance came across as a lack of trust in everyone in her company. Leah never really became close with the rest of us. The three of us at the club, who were open and vulnerable, stayed friends for many years, while Leah, by keeping up a wall, made it hard to build a real connection and eventually disappeared from our group.

On the other hand, my friend Renata became especially dear to me. She would joke about her "less than exemplary" mothering skills or tell us about the latest domestic dispute with her husband. We were able to laugh because we could all relate to the challenges that come with family interactions, and in sharing these relatable struggles, she let us see her as she was—real, imperfect, and authentic.

I'm not saying that we need to divulge every little detail about our lives with all our acquaintances or colleagues, but there is something to be said about what leadership author Patrick Lencioni calls *vulnerability-based trust.* In relationships, especially those that matter to us, by revealing our own struggles or imperfections, we invite others to do the same, as there is a feeling that we've been given something valuable.

Being vulnerable takes courage, whether it's admitting you don't have an answer, sharing a concern, or asking for help. Vulnerability makes us more human and relatable because everyone knows what it's like to feel unsure or in need of support. Leah didn't connect with us in this way, and without that openness, it felt like she kept a part of herself hidden, which made it hard to form a lasting bond.

Lencioni underscores this idea of vulnerability-based trust as a foundation for strong teams. Vulnerability is transformative since it changes the way we see and interact with one another, especially in relationships that require collaboration and mutual support. In my interaction with Jack, a drastic change took place after I opened up and shared how his late response affected me. By letting him know,

I showed vulnerability while communicating with empathy, assuming his positive intent.

Being vulnerable takes courage, but it fosters trust in many ways. When we're open about challenges, we show authenticity, which makes us more relatable. Vulnerability also encourages reciprocity because when one person shares openly, it creates space for others to do the same. It helps level the playing field, dismantling power imbalances, and most importantly, it builds psychological safety, where people feel free to express themselves without fear of judgment.

Leaders who embrace vulnerability set the tone for a culture of trust, making collaboration smoother and relationships more resilient.

Elements of Trust

Trust in professional relationships is built intentionally over time. The more we know people, the more we trust or don't trust them. Different elements need to be present for trust to flourish. In their book, *The Trusted Advisor*, Charles H. Green, David Maister, and Robert M. Galford developed a "trust equation" [12] which breaks down the components of trustworthiness into a practical formula. Whether you're a fan of formulas or not, their trust equation offers a helpful perspective on what makes us trust certain people more than others.

---

[12] David H. Maister, Charles H. Green, and Robert M. Galford, *The Trusted Advisor* (New York: Free Press, 2001).

Trust Equation

$$TQ = \frac{\text{Credibility} + \text{Reliability} + \text{Intimacy}}{\text{Self Orientation}}$$

Let's break down each element:

Credibility

Credibility refers to a person's knowledge, expertise, and ability to perform a task. It's about knowing our stuff, being transparent, and staying consistent in our decisions. It's easier to trust those who show competence and communicate clearly and confidently.

A product manager, for example, may explain the technical trade-offs in plain language, making sure everyone, both engineers and non-engineers, understand the stakes. When introducing a roadmap, they can connect it to past performance and data, so it doesn't feel like guesswork, promoting trust because they bring expertise in a way that helps others feel aligned.

Reliability

Reliability is all about following through on commitments. When someone says they'll do something, and they do it, we learn to trust them.

There's something very important about never overpromising. For example, if we say that a report will be ready Thursday, we need to make sure it is, without reminders or last-minute scrambles. Knowing what's coming without drama or surprises increases trustworthiness because there's never a need to save the day.

Intimacy

Intimacy in this context has nothing to do with romance; it's about the level of safety we feel in confiding personal or sensitive matters. People are more likely to trust those with whom they feel secure and respected, knowing that what they share will be treated with discretion.

If, for example, someone is struggling and yet we listen to them without rushing them or if we can ask thoughtful questions and make sure that what they shared stays private, we're creating intimacy. People naturally open up to certain people about doubts, burnout or insecurities.

Self-Orientation

Self-orientation is the denominator of the equation. A high degree of self-orientation, where someone seems focused on their own agenda, can erode everything built up in the numerator. People are less likely to trust someone who seems more interested in their success than in the team's goals.

If someone is too focused on their own ideas or constantly one-upping others, self-orientation becomes evident and decreases the level of trust. Behaviors like interrupting, redirecting conversations or highlighting our contributions can make others pull back.

The trust equation highlights credibility, reliability, and intimacy, balanced against self-orientation. But it's the element of intimacy that especially paves the way for deeper trust through vulnerability.

Vulnerability-based trust goes a step further, requiring us to show our true selves, including our weaknesses and fears. This kind of trust fosters a more authentic connection, one that's essential for building strong, resilient teams. When leaders embrace vulnerability, they help create a culture in which people feel safe to contribute, share ideas, and take risks.

Building Trust By Being There

In any relationship, showing up for others is essential for building trust. Steve, a new project manager at an insurance wholesale brokerage company was tasked with launching a project to consolidate the agency management system and he had only a two-day transition period from his predecessor before he was expected to hit the ground running. Soon after he started, his testers in Europe reported major software issues, while he was already being pulled in multiple directions.

Steve's first impulse was to put them off and focus on other priorities. But he didn't ignore them. He listened to their challenges and got a high-caliber expert to help with a fresh approach by starting in a new environment. As launch time neared, his commitment paid off, and they were able to launch the project in record time. Those testers were very grateful and motivated to move the project forward.

Stories such as Steve's remind us that being there for others also builds trust. These small, consistent actions show others that we're reliable and committed to the team's success. And while the digital age has reshaped the way we connect; it hasn't changed our basic human need for trust in relationships.

Summary: The Knots That Break Teams

Conflict is an inevitable part of life, but when emotions take over, it can escalate quickly. When I had my road rage incident in Mexico City, what started as a minor incident spiraled into an intense showdown, all thanks to what psychologists call an amygdala hijack.

In the workplace, these emotional reactions can manifest when we feel our competence, reputation, or even identity is under attack. Without pausing to consider other perspectives, we can get stuck in a cycle of reaction and defensiveness. This kind of unchecked conflict not only damages relationships but also undermines collaboration and trust.

Trust is the backbone of any strong team or relationship, but it's fragile and easily eroded. When people don't feel safe to express themselves or fear judgment, they retreat. The absence of trust creates barriers to honest conversations, leaving misunderstandings unresolved and tensions simmering under the surface.

Untangling the Knots

The key to navigating conflict and building trust lies in shifting our mindset and approach. The following three strategies can untangle these challenges:

Pause and Reframe: Instead of reacting impulsively, pause to consider the other person's perspective. Ask yourself, "What could be going on with them?" This moment of reflection can diffuse tension and turn a potential clash into an opportunity for understanding.

Build Trust Through Vulnerability: Trust grows when people feel safe and supported. Sharing a bit of yourself creates the kind of vulnerability that deepens connections. Showing up, following through, and giving others the benefit of the doubt reinforces that trust over time.

Embrace Honest Conversations: Trust opens the door to meaningful dialogue, even about difficult topics. By creating an environment of psychological safety, teams can engage in honest, constructive conversations. These discussions help resolve tensions and strengthen relationships, making conflict a tool for growth rather than a source of division.

Conflict and feedback go hand in hand. A lot of workplace tension arises not because people disagree, but because they don't know how to express those disagreements or observations constructively. Giving and receiving feedback the right way can transform relationships and drive real progress.

Average players want to be left alone. Good players want to be coached. Great players want to be told the truth.

— **Doc Rivers**

CHAPTER 3

Feedback in Communication

Trauma-Free Feedback

When I was in kindergarten, a dental hygienist came to give a presentation on dental care. Holding a large model of teeth and a huge toothbrush, she asked whether anyone wanted to demonstrate how to brush their teeth. A few of us raised our hands and I was picked. I stood up shyly, took the toothbrush, and began to rub it side to side on the teeth. "No, that's wrong!" she said, and took the brush from me. I walked back to my place, my face burning and thoroughly humiliated as I felt the weight of the other children's pitying looks.

How is it that I can remember this tiny piece of my life that happened an eternity ago and not much more? I can still feel the shame at being singled out in front of my peers. To say the hygienist was not very good at giving feedback would have been an understatement. She was so focused on the task that she didn't think of how her public chiding would make me feel.

She could have gently guided my hand to show me the correct stroke and encouraged me. Instead, her actions left me ashamed, resentful and regretting that I had volunteered. I was so mortified that I couldn't pay attention to the rest of the presentation, and I don't think I changed my brushing technique. What a wasted opportunity. That was my first experience with bad feedback in the real world.

This likely explains why so many of my clients admit that when they hear the word feedback, they can't help but cringe and brace themselves for what they expect will be a reprimand or criticism. Feedback is associated with an unpleasant experience, and for all the talk about how crucial it should be considered in our development, I have yet to find real excitement about receiving feedback.

Redefining Feedback

Let's take a step back and consider what feedback is truly meant to be. At its core, feedback is information given in response to an action, behavior, or performance, designed to help people understand the impact of their actions and either adjust or continue positive behaviors.

Recognition feedback celebrates what we're doing well. More than empty praise, it should be a specific, sincere acknowledgment of effective actions. Recognition feedback tells people that their efforts are seen and valued, reinforcing behaviors that contribute positively.

Corrective feedback, on the other hand, is intended to guide someone toward improvement. Rather than merely pointing out mistakes, it provides clear, constructive suggestions to help someone grow and succeed. When delivered thoughtfully, corrective feedback offers the insights needed to adjust without diminishing confidence.

Good feedback, whether recognition or corrective, is clear, specific, and timely, providing insights that promote growth, learning, and encouragement. It's a tool for building mutual understanding and fostering development, aligning people more closely with shared goals or values in both personal and professional settings.

How often do most of us associate feedback with encouragement? Probably not too often. Yet, the most impactful feedback genuinely motivates change and reinforces good habits. Giving feedback that creates constructive empowerment with a real value proposition transforms it from something people dread into a vital, supportive tool for growth.

The Cost of Zero Feedback

When I was designing a leadership program for operations managers at a construction materials company, one issue surfaced repeatedly: high turnover. Many managers confided that they often avoided giving feedback, unsure of the best timing, tone, or approach. Some worried about creating tension if they gave corrective feedback; others feared it might backfire or reduce morale. So, many of them simply put it off. Instead of addressing performance issues early, they'd let frustrations build until their only solution seemed to let someone go.

When HR asked what corrective actions had been taken to help the employee improve, managers often admitted that no structured feedback or guidance had been given. They felt uncomfortable with those conversations, and without the right tools or strategies, allowed issues to simmer and grow. This led to a cycle where employees were often blindsided by abrupt, stressful confrontations when managers reached their breaking point. These heated moments or sudden terminations left employees feeling unsupported and demoralized, causing some to leave on their own.

Over time, this pattern of avoidance followed by crisis became a major contributor to turnover and a culture of mistrust. The lack of proactive feedback and guidance highlighted a critical gap: Without timely, constructive feedback, both employees and managers were left feeling disconnected, and the organization suffered as a result. This type of environment highlights the importance of integrating regular, meaningful recognition into feedback processes, making it a priority rather than an afterthought.

Once the managers learned how to structure feedback and felt more confident in its delivery, they saw a decrease in turnover and surprisingly were also able to quantify the time they were saving (an average of 10 hours per week), since they no longer had to repeat themselves or take on tasks previously delegated to team members. Culture is fostered by the leaders, so if organizations want to see a culture of recognition and constructive and constant feedback, leaders need to model the behavior.

Recognition that Resonates

Once, during a coaching session for a client partner, I was asked to find a meeting room within a specified budget at the hotel where I was staying. When I arrived, I noticed an unused, large meeting room and inquired about borrowing it. Although they initially quoted a fee, I was able to persuade them to let me use it at no cost. I informed my client partner of the savings and assured them there was no need for reimbursement.

A week later, I received a thoughtful email from my client, expressing appreciation for my proactive approach in saving them money and recognizing my commitment to our partnership. That simple gesture of recognition touched me. I felt valued, and it reinforced my own dedication to the work we were doing together.

It's easy to underestimate the power of a simple "Thank you." But in workplace settings, these small acts of recognition can carry so much weight. Gallup has studied employee engagement for decades, and their findings establish that recognition plays a crucial role in employee morale, productivity, and overall satisfaction. In fact, Gallup's poll reveals that employees who receive regular recognition are more likely to stay with their organization,[13] work harder, and feel more connected to their work.

Yet if we look at the typical workplace, we find that recognition often takes a backseat. It's something reserved for formal performance reviews or special occasions, not part of everyday culture. Gallup's data shows that only about one-third of employees feel they receive adequate recognition at work.

Imagine that: Two-thirds of employees are moving through their workday without knowing whether their contributions are valued. This gap is a missed opportunity, as recognizing good work is one of the most effective and easiest ways to boost engagement and morale.

When we talk about feedback, we often focus solely on the corrective side, but feedback is incomplete without recognition. It's an acknowledgment of a person's contribution, in essence saying, "What you do matters." And when you think of our virtual and often impersonal work environments, these words can carry enormous weight.

---

[13] Gallup, "U.S. Employee Engagement Inches Up Slightly After 11-Year Low," July 26, 2024.

If we look at this from a psychological perspective, beginning with Frederick Herzberg's Motivation-Hygiene Theory in the 1950s, it revealed that job satisfaction and dissatisfaction arise from two different sets of factors. Hygiene factors, such as salary, job security, and working conditions, prevent dissatisfaction but don't necessarily motivate employees to go above and beyond. Motivators, on the other hand, drive higher satisfaction, creativity, and commitment, and among these, recognition ranks high.

Herzberg argued that recognition is fundamental to motivation. When employees feel their efforts are acknowledged, they're more likely to find meaning and pride in their work. They're motivated to contribute and innovate more. Recognition becomes essential for creating a workplace where people develop a sense of belonging and want to be.

If we go even further back, we can trace the importance of recognition to Abraham Maslow's Hierarchy of Needs. Maslow's model suggests that humans strive to fulfill certain levels of need, from the basics of survival up to self-actualization. Near the top of this hierarchy is the need for esteem, which includes both self-respect and the respect and recognition of others.

Building on Maslow's ideas, Self-Determination Theory (SDT), developed by Edward Deci and Richard Ryan, shows how recognition impacts motivation. SDT identifies three core psychological needs that drive motivation and engagement: autonomy, competence, and relatedness. Recognition plays a critical role in satisfying two of these needs: competence and relatedness. [14]

Competence: When employees receive specific, positive feedback that acknowledges their skills or accomplishments, they feel a sense of mastery and achievement. This reinforces their belief in their ability to perform effectively, encouraging them to take on new challenges and grow professionally.

Relatedness: Recognition fosters connection and mutual respect between employees and their leaders or peers. By showing that an individual's contributions are noticed and valued, recognition strengthens interpersonal bonds, creating a sense of inclusion and belonging within the workplace.

Deci and Ryan argue that motivation flourishes when these psychological needs are met. Recognition, as part of regular feedback, satisfies both the need to feel capable (competence) and the need to feel connected to others (relatedness). Without recognition, employees are more likely to feel disengaged and disconnected, regardless of how fulfilling other aspects of their job may be.

When we blend all these findings, we arrive at a simple reality: Recognition can be an indispensable tool for leaders because it addresses both the human need for esteem and the intrinsic drivers of motivation. Recognition transforms tasks from mere obligations into meaningful contributions, helping individuals and teams thrive.

---

[14] Edward L. Deci and Richard M. Ryan, *Intrinsic Motivation and Self-Determination in Human Behavior* (New York: Springer, 1985).

I've had a few clients ask, "Why should I recognize people for doing their job?" Don't get me wrong. I'm not suggesting tickling people's ears with empty flattery, since that would devalue the purpose of positive feedback and ultimately, inauthenticity is counterproductive. I know that some people have very high standards for themselves and may transfer those expectations to others, but it's important to be honest. Even high achievers thrive under the recognition of a job well done. A sincere word of appreciation goes a long way.

> Even high achievers thrive under the recognition of a job well done.

Yet, knowing that recognition is vital isn't enough. How recognition is given matters just as much as why. When recognition is specific and tied to meaningful outcomes, it becomes far more impactful. There's a simple framework called CARE that can make this easier.

The CARE Model for Recognition Feedback

CARE is a straightforward, yet versatile framework designed to make recognition feedback clear, meaningful, and actionable. Its three steps—**Context & Action, Result**, and **Effect**—ensure feedback is both specific and supportive, empowering people to replicate success and feel genuinely appreciated.

While recognition feedback might seem simple, it's often mishandled. Many people believe a quick "Great job!" is enough, but vague or incomplete feedback misses an opportunity to reinforce positive behaviors effectively.

For instance, consider a manager saying, "You handled yesterday's crunch really well." While this is intended as praise, it leaves the receiver guessing: *What exactly did I do well? Was it how I managed my time? Was it how I collaborated with the team?*

Recognition feedback loses its power when it lacks specificity and fails to connect the person's actions to their broader impact. The CARE model can help us with that. Let's break down each step and why it's crucial to the process.

1. Context & Action

We should start by describing the context or situation and the specific action the individual took. Providing clear context ensures the feedback is precise and eliminates ambiguity. The clarity highlights the specific actions that led to the recognition.

This step is focused on facts, using neutral and objective language. It helps to avoid adding subjective opinions or premature judgments. Neutral language also makes the feedback more grounded. At this stage, we haven't yet discussed why the action mattered — that comes later.

Example:

"During last week's team meeting, when there was some confusion, you stepped in to clarify the project timeline."

2. Result

Next, we should explain the immediate outcome of the action. What was achieved because of the individual's action or behavior? The result should be tangible and directly linked to their effort, highlighting the cause-and-effect relationship.

This step helps connect their actions to visible or measurable outcomes. By showing this connection, feedback becomes more purposeful and motivating. This step also sets the stage for discussing the broader effect in the next step.

Example:

"Your clarification kept the discussion on track and ensured everyone left with a clear understanding of their deadlines."

3. Effect

Finally, it's important to explain the broader significance of their action. This step is often overlooked in recognition feedback, but it's the most powerful part.

This step answers the critical question: Why does this matter? It goes beyond the immediate result to show how their contribution impacted the team, project, or organization. Highlighting the broader effect not only shows appreciation but also provides motivation by connecting their effort to a larger purpose.

It reinforces the importance of their contribution and inspires them to continue similar behaviors in the future.

Example:

"Your initiative helped maintain the team's momentum. It made a big impact on ensuring everyone stayed aligned and productive."

Through these three steps, the CARE model helps ensure recognition feedback is precise, meaningful, and inspiring. It shows people not only what they've done well but also why it mattered, fostering motivation and continued excellence.

Here's how the CARE model works in practice:
Context & Action:

"During last week's team meeting, when there was some confusion, you stepped in to clarify the project timeline."

Result:

"This kept the discussion on track and ensured everyone left with a clear understanding of their deadlines."

Effect:

"Your initiative made a big difference in maintaining the team's momentum and productivity."

Note how this contrasts a basic statement of praise such as "Great job during the meeting!" Now you've got a recognition statement with substance and strength that will land with much more power.

When done right, recognition feedback builds trust and reinforces positive behaviors. It's a tool that everyone can use to inspire excellence and create a culture where contributions are genuinely valued.

But not every feedback conversation is about recognizing success. What do we do when we want someone to stop doing something or change an action or behavior? We will want to speak in a way that encourages growth and collaboration. Let's look at a different model, which I call FRAME. It's designed to help guide corrective feedback conversations, ensuring they are clear, constructive, and motivating.

The FRAME Model for Corrective Feedback

Corrective feedback is one of the hardest conversations to get right. Unlike recognition feedback, which feels natural and uplifting, corrective feedback carries the weight of potential discomfort for both the giver and the receiver. As we saw at the construction materials company, many leaders avoid it altogether for fear of hurting someone's feelings while others jump in too quickly, letting frustration or criticism take over. Both approaches miss the mark.

If we want corrective feedback to land in a way that drives real change, we need to approach it with care and clarity. Part of the reason we often hesitate to give it is that we're afraid of hurting or humiliating someone (like that dental hygienist did to me).

The first and most important step is starting with the right frame of mind (remember our earlier discussion on emotional intelligence) and ensuring that our intent is focused on helping the other person grow, not just venting our frustrations or pointing out mistakes.

During my project with the construction materials company, I had to work with managers to make sure they addressed the issue that needed to be corrected in a timely manner, though I cautioned them not to act directly afterward if the situation had made them angry.

Think about it. If you let things go because you hope to avoid an unpleasant conversation, but then the situation seems to get worse, you risk feeling angry or letting things become personal, and what may have started as a simple feedback conversation can escalate into a full-blown conflict. Before jumping into a feedback conversation, it's vital to start with the right head space and that requires a little bit of reflection. It's essential to ask ourselves:

- What behavior or outcome do I want to change?
- Why is this change important?
- Am I delivering this feedback to genuinely help the other person succeed?

When we approach corrective feedback with the right mindset, it becomes less about criticism and more about collaboration. The goal is to help the other person see what went wrong, understand its impact, and align on how to move forward constructively. When corrective feedback is delivered well, it strengthens relationships, builds trust, and leads to better outcomes instead of resentment or defensiveness.

The FRAME model provides a structured, step-by-step approach to giving corrective feedback that is clear, constructive, and results driven. It ensures that feedback is grounded in facts and focused on positive outcomes. You can tailor it to the leadership style you choose to adopt, be it either more directive or collaborative. Let's take a closer look at how the model works.

F—Facts: Describe Reality

The first step in the FRAME model is to focus on the facts, to describe the situation and the specific action taken (or not taken). This step is fundamental because it establishes a common understanding of what happened.

At this stage, your goal is simply to state the facts clearly so both you and the other person are aligned before moving forward. Without this foundation, it's easy for misunderstandings to derail the feedback before it even begins.

It's tempting to start with a value judgment, especially if you feel frustrated. But words like "uncommitted" or "distracted" carry emotional weight that can make the listener feel judged or attacked. Even with the best intentions, language like this can cause defensiveness.

The moment they feel criticized, the listener may tune out, become defensive, or even dismiss your feedback entirely. They may start justifying their actions internally and think, *They've already made up their mind about me. Forget it!* And once defensiveness sets in, it's hard to bring the conversation back to a constructive place.

Neutral language, by contrast, keeps the listener engaged. It creates a sense of safety and trust, making it easier for them to follow your feedback. At this stage, you're not evaluating or drawing conclusions; you're simply inviting them to see the same facts as you. It's like guiding someone through a map. If you jump straight to the destination without showing the route, they'll likely get lost. But if you take it step by step, they'll stay with you.

Let's look at how your approach can make or break this step:

What Not to Do

Imagine starting a conversation like this:

"You completely messed up the timeline during yesterday's presentation. It made us look unprofessional in front of the client."

What's your gut reaction to something like this? Does it feel grating? Words such as "messed up" and "unprofessional" sound judgmental and are emotionally charged, which may trigger defensiveness. There also seems to be an assumption of intent. Phrases such as "you completely" imply blame without considering what might have led to the situation. Lastly, there's no clarity about what was incorrect or why it mattered.

What impact could this have on the listener? They might feel attacked and think, *They're not even giving me a chance to explain!* This shuts down dialogue and creates resistance, making it harder to move forward.

What to Do Instead

Now consider this alternative:

Facts:

"During yesterday's client presentation, the timeline you shared didn't align with the latest project updates."

Notice the difference? This statement is neutral and objective. It sticks to the facts without adding blame or emotional language and it's specific enough for the listener to understand exactly what is being referenced. By focusing on what happened rather than assigning intent, you invite a conversation instead of creating defensiveness.

With this approach, the receiver is more likely to think, *Okay, that's true. Let's figure out what happened and how to fix it.* This keeps the conversation collaborative and focused.

Why does this matter? Well, when you stick to the facts, you set the tone for a constructive conversation. You give the listener a reason to stay with you rather than bristle at perceived criticism. At this stage, you're not making judgments or revealing the impact of their actions—that will come later. For now, you're setting the context by referencing the facts of the situation.

By focusing on the facts, you create a strong foundation for the next stages of the FRAME model, where you'll explore the results and work toward solutions.

R—Result: Explain the Impact

You've described the situation and facts surrounding it. Now it's time to explain the immediate outcome of the action (or inaction). Did it create extra work for the team? Confuse a client? Delay a project? This step helps the listener understand why the issue matters without assigning blame or jumping to conclusions about their intent. The goal is to create understanding, not defensiveness.

Highlighting the result is essential because it links the person's behavior to its consequences. This connection fosters accountability and understanding, making the feedback more purposeful and actionable. Without this step, the feedback may feel incomplete or arbitrary, leaving the receiver wondering, *Why is this such a big deal?*

At the same time, it's important to avoid overwhelming them with overly broad or catastrophic descriptions. Your goal here is to focus on the immediate, specific result, keeping the conversation constructive and actionable.

What Not to Do

Imagine starting a conversation like this:

"Because of your mistake, the whole project is now behind schedule. You've caused a lot of unnecessary work for everyone."

This approach might feel justified in the heat of the moment, but words such as "mistake" and "unnecessary work" sound accusatory and emotionally charged, which can put the listener on the defensive. Phrasing it as "your mistake" also implies fault without considering any external factors that might have contributed to the issue. Also, saying "the whole project is now behind schedule" is too broad and overwhelming. It doesn't provide clarity about what specifically went wrong or how it affected the team.

How might this be perceived? The listener could feel attacked or scapegoated, thinking, *This isn't entirely my fault—they're blowing it out of proportion.* This reaction makes them less likely to engage with feedback or take accountability.

What to Do Instead
Result:

Now let's look at a better approach:

"This caused confusion for the client and led to additional follow-up work for the team."

Notice the difference? This version sticks to the facts while clearly outlining the immediate result. The language is neutral and avoids blame or assumptions. Instead of overwhelming the listener, it focuses on a specific impact, which was client confusion and the need for follow-up work. This approach keeps the conversation constructive and collaborative.

The receiver is more likely to think, *Oh…I see how my action caused this issue.* By connecting actions to outcomes in a clear and objective way, you encourage accountability and openness.

When you explain the impact, you help the other person see the connection between their behavior and its consequences. This shifts the conversation from what happened to why it matters. It's this connection that makes feedback meaningful and actionable. Without it, the feedback might feel arbitrary, leaving the receiver unsure of its importance or how to improve.

At the same time, stay focused on the immediate result. Overstating the impact with broad or emotional language can overwhelm the listener and shut down the conversation. Specific, tangible outcomes are easier to understand and address.

Keep Going! Don't Pause or Open the Conversation Up Just Yet!

Here's where many people get tripped up: After describing the result, it's tempting to open the conversation by asking for the other person's thoughts or perspective. For example, after stating, "This caused confusion for the client and led to additional follow-up work for the team," you might instinctively follow with, "What happened?" While this may seem like an invitation for dialogue, it can backfire.

Why? Because at this stage, the receiver may feel the need to justify their actions or defend themselves. They could begin shifting blame, pointing out other factors that contributed to the situation, or even shutting down defensively. Instead of staying focused on the facts and the result, the conversation risks veering into unproductive territory. Once defensiveness enters the discussion, it's much harder to realign the conversation toward solutions.

To avoid this, it's better to hold off on opening the conversation until you reach the alignment step. The alignment stage provides the opportunity to introduce the desired alternative result, which is the outcome you want, and shift the discussion toward future improvement. By moving towards the positive outcome without dwelling too much on the negative, you maintain control of the narrative and keep the conversation constructive. The receiver will be less likely to feel judged and more likely to focus on collaborating toward a better outcome.

At this stage, our role is to ensure understanding of the facts and the results, not to start troubleshooting or asking for explanations. We should keep the conversation steady and clear. The listener doesn't need to respond to the result just yet; they simply need to absorb it. This approach reduces defensiveness and sets the stage for a smoother, more productive alignment step.

By clearly stating the result and holding off on opening the discussion, we create a foundation for the next step in the FRAME model: aligning on the desired outcome and exploring actionable solutions. This sequence ensures the feedback conversation remains purposeful, focused, and solution driven.

Align: Clarify the Objective

After describing the facts and explaining the result, the next step is to clarify the objective. This is where we introduce the why of the feedback: What alternative outcome are we aiming for, and why does it matter? By clearly stating the desired result and its significance, we help the receiver see where the conversation is headed and why their role in achieving this goal is essential.

This stage is about creating a shared vision of what success looks like, whether it's improving team efficiency, meeting stakeholder expectations, or ensuring smoother processes. It shifts the focus from what went wrong to what can go right, providing a forward-looking tone that motivates the receiver. When done well, alignment establishes a sense of purpose and sets the stage for collaboration.

What Not to Do

Imagine saying this:

"You need to do a better job next time, so this doesn't happen again. It's unacceptable that the client left feeling confused."

At first glance, this might seem like you're addressing the problem, but let's unpack why this approach falls short. The phrase "do a better job" is vague and leaves the listener guessing about what "better" looks like. Words such as "unacceptable" are emotionally charged and more likely to provoke defensiveness than cooperation. Finally, this statement fails to connect the feedback to a broader purpose, since it doesn't explain why clarity is crucial or how it benefits the client and the team.

How might this land with the listener? They may feel criticized or demoralized, thinking, *They're pointing out what's wrong but not telling me what's expected*. Without a clear objective, it's hard for them to move forward constructively, leaving both parties frustrated.

What to Do Instead

Now consider this alternative:

Align:

"We want to ensure that clients leave our presentations with a clear and accurate understanding of the timeline to build trust and help streamline follow-up efforts."

This approach works because it paints a clear picture of what success looks like, namely, clients feeling confident and informed. It ties the feedback to a specific purpose, showing why the desired outcome matters for both the individual and the organization. Instead of lingering on the mistake, it focuses on a shared goal, encouraging the receiver to think, "I see what's expected, and I understand why it's important."

This phrasing also removes judgment or blame, keeping the tone collaborative and forward focused. The listener is more likely to feel motivated to meet the objective rather than stuck dwelling on what went wrong.

Clarifying the objective provides direction and purpose. If you skip it, feedback can feel critical or aimless, leaving the receiver unsure of what's expected or how to improve. When you clearly articulate the desired result, you help the other person connect their efforts to a bigger picture, showing them how their role contributes to success.

Alignment is also an opportunity to reframe the conversation. Rather than focusing on what didn't work, we're collaborating to achieve a better outcome. This subtle shift in tone transforms feedback into a constructive discussion, making it easier to transition into actionable solutions.

With a clear objective established, the conversation is now ready to move into the next phase: mapping out actionable solutions. By aligning with the desired result first, we ensure that we are both working toward the same goal, paving the way for a constructive and productive dialogue.

M — Map: Collaborate on Actionable Steps

Once we've clarified the objective, the next step is to map out actionable solutions. This stage is where we transition from discussing the problem to exploring how to achieve the desired outcome. But how we approach this step can vary depending on our leadership style and the situation at hand.

In some cases, a directive approach may be most effective. This involves laying out a specific course of action for the receiver to follow. By clearly stipulating what needs to be done, we remove ambiguity and provide a concrete plan. This can be particularly useful when time is limited, the receiver lacks experience in the area, or when the situation requires immediate corrective action.

On the other hand, a coaching or collaborative approach invites the receiver to participate in generating solutions. Instead of prescribing an alternative action, we can ask open-ended questions to encourage them to think critically and propose their own solutions. This style can be especially powerful for fostering commitment, as it gives the receiver ownership of the solution rather than simply following instructions. It also turns the feedback conversation into a development opportunity, helping the receiver build problem-solving skills and take accountability for their actions.

Both approaches have their advantages, and the choice depends on factors such as the urgency of the situation, the receiver's level of experience, and our overall goals for the conversation. The key is to adapt our method to the context while ensuring the solutions are clear, actionable, and aligned with the objective.

What Not to Do

Consider this approach:

"You need to fix this by the next meeting, or it's going to cause a bigger problem."

While this might seem to address urgency, it leaves much to be desired. First, it doesn't provide any direction on how to fix the issue. Phrasing such as "it's going to cause a bigger problem" adds pressure without offering clarity or support. Additionally, this statement is directive without being constructive, since it demands a result but doesn't give the receiver the tools or opportunity to work toward it.

How might this come across to the listener? They may feel overwhelmed or unsupported, thinking, *I'm being told to fix it, but I don't even know where to start.* Without clear guidance or collaboration, feedback like that carries the risk of being ineffective or even counterproductive.

What to Do Instead

Now consider this:

Map:
(Directive Style)

"Let's review the project timeline together before the next client meeting to ensure alignment. I'll also send you a checklist of updates to verify against before presenting."

This approach provides clear, specific instructions. It stipulates the exact actions the receiver should take, leaving little room for ambiguity. It's practical for situations where immediate results are needed or where the receiver may lack the experience to generate effective solutions independently.

Map:
(Coaching Style)

"What do you suggest we do to ensure the timeline is fully aligned with the latest updates before the next client meeting?"

This style uses open-ended questions to encourage the receiver to reflect and come up with solutions. It promotes ownership and accountability while turning feedback into a developmental opportunity. This approach is particularly effective for team member development, building long-term skills and fostering a collaborative environment.

This step is where feedback becomes actionable. Without mapping solutions, the conversation may feel incomplete, leaving the receiver unsure of how to improve. Providing clear, specific next steps ensures that the feedback translates into progress, while involving the receiver in the process reinforces accountability and collaboration.

At the same time, mapping solutions allows us to tailor the approach to the situation. If a more directive style is needed, we can present a concrete plan. If the situation calls for a coaching approach, open-ended questions can encourage the receiver to think critically and offer their own ideas. By adapting our method, we ensure that the feedback resonates and drives results.

With actionable solutions in place, the feedback conversation is ready to move into the final stage: engagement. This step focuses on confirming understanding and commitment. By mapping solutions first, we've set the foundation for a collaborative and productive resolution.

E — Engage: Confirm Understanding and Commitment

The final step in the FRAME model is engagement: ensuring that the feedback conversation ends with clear understanding and a mutual commitment to the next steps. This step is about closing the loop. It's not enough to describe the facts, explain the result, align on the objective, and map solutions; we need to confirm we're on the same page and ready to move forward.

Engagement ensures that the feedback conversation translates into action. It gives the receiver the opportunity to clarify any points of confusion, voice concerns, or seek additional support. It also emphasizes accountability, as the receiver explicitly agrees to follow through on the solutions discussed. This step strengthens the partnership between both parties, showing that you are invested in their success.

What Not to Do

Imagine ending the conversation like this:

"Okay, so you'll fix this moving forward, right?"

While this might seem like a simple way to wrap things up, it leaves too much to chance. The phrasing is vague and doesn't invite the receiver to articulate their understanding or commitment. It also doesn't provide space for the receiver to ask questions or express any challenges they might foresee.

How might this land with the listener? They might nod along without fully grasping expectations or feel pressured to agree without genuinely committing to the plan. This can lead to misunderstandings, incomplete follow-through, or unresolved issues down the line.

What to Do Instead

Try this approach instead:

Engage:

"Does this plan make sense to you? Do you feel comfortable moving forward with the steps we discussed? Is there anything you'd like to adjust or discuss further before we move ahead?"

This phrasing works because it's clear, collaborative, and supportive. By asking open-ended questions, we give the receiver the chance to confirm their understanding and express any concerns. It ensures that they are not only aware of the next steps but also actively invested in executing them. This approach strengthens accountability and fosters a sense of partnership.

The receiver is more likely to think, *I understand what's expected, and I feel ready to take the next steps.* This leaves the conversation on a positive and proactive note.

Engagement is the final piece of the puzzle. Without it, even the best feedback conversation can lose its effectiveness. Confirming understanding and commitment ensures that the solutions discussed are actionable and realistic, leaving no room for misinterpretation. It also reinforces accountability by explicitly asking the receiver to agree to the plan and gives us a chance to identify any potential barriers early, so we can address them together before they become obstacles.

Bringing the FRAME Model Together

With engagement, the feedback conversation comes full circle. We've described the facts, explained the result, aligned the objective, mapped actionable solutions, and confirmed commitment. By ending the conversation with a shared understanding and mutual agreement, we ensure that the feedback moves from discussion to a clear roadmap that points us in the right direction.

Let's see how the FRAME model works in a real feedback conversation. Each step builds on the previous one, creating a clear, constructive, and actionable dialogue:

F - Focus on the Facts:

"During yesterday's client presentation, the timeline you shared didn't align with the latest project updates."

R - Explain the Result:

"This caused confusion for the client and led to additional follow-up work for the team." *(don't stop or pause here)*

A - Align the Objective:

"We want to ensure that clients leave our presentations with a clear and accurate understanding of the timeline to build trust and help streamline follow-up effort."

M - Map Solutions:

Directive Approach: "Let's review the project timeline together before the next client meeting to ensure alignment. I'll also send you a checklist of updates to verify against before presenting."

Coaching Approach: "What do you suggest we do to ensure the timeline is fully aligned with the latest updates before the next client meeting?"

E - Confirm Engagement:

"Does this plan make sense to you? Do you feel comfortable moving forward with the steps we discussed? Is there anything you'd like to adjust or discuss further before we move ahead?"

Notice how each step flows naturally into the next. The conversation starts with facts to create alignment, introduces the result to connect actions to outcomes, clarifies the objective to set a shared goal, maps out actionable solutions, and concludes with engagement to ensure understanding and commitment.

A Framework for Constructive Feedback

The FRAME model makes delivering feedback easier and is a guide for fostering collaboration and growth. It can be useful not only in a work environment, but in our everyday interactions as well. Let's again review my unpleasant experience with the dental hygienist, which, had she used the FRAME model, might have sounded something like this:

(F) "I notice you're brushing the teeth from side to side."

(R) "Though that may seem like the easiest way to brush all your teeth, it misses the gums that are on top that may have food hidden underneath them." *(no pause, keep going)*

(A) "We want to make sure we cover them too, since we don't want problems like cavities appearing later."

(M) "Let me show you how to brush from top to bottom by guiding your hand while you brush."

(or)

"How do you think you need to brush so you can get to the hidden food under the gums?"

(E) "Great! How does that feel? Do you think you can brush your teeth like this from now on?"

I can tell you without a doubt that had this been feedback I received, I would not be mulling over my hurt feelings so many decades later and I probably would have been more consistent with my dental hygiene! This simple framework is effective because it considers the other person's dignity and delivers feedback in a spirit of goodwill and collaboration. You can try it with your loved ones too!

By following these steps, we ensure that our feedback conversations are purposeful, clear, and actionable. We can see that each step serves a distinct purpose. Focusing on the facts grounds the discussion, explaining the result emphasizes why the feedback matters, clarifying the objective provides direction, mapping solutions ensures progress, and confirming engagement solidifies commitment.

When used consistently, the FRAME model transforms feedback from a dreaded conversation into a constructive exchange. It helps drive better outcomes while also strengthening relationships and motivating teams to work together. The FRAME model gives you a straightforward way to make these conversations meaningful.

Receiving Feedback

A client of mine, a delivery manager, told me of a situation where she sat through a project review meeting and felt her chest tighten the moment the project manager blurted out, "You guys always do this! There's always something!" The vague statement landed like an accusatory and unfair slap. Her team had been working hard to stay on track, but now, all their efforts seemed diminished to an undefined "this."

In that instant, she could feel the reaction rising: defensiveness, frustration, and the urge to snap back. It's a common story: feedback delivered poorly, phrased in a way that triggers emotions instead of inviting solutions. It feels like someone just dumped a handful of messy, irritating dirt into your hands.

> Feedback delivered poorly feels like someone just dumped dirt in your hands.

But I tell my clients, if you dig a little deeper, beneath that dirt, there's often something useful like a seed of insight that can help you grow. The real skill lies in recognizing it, finding it, and deciding how to nurture it.

Poorly delivered feedback can feel vague ("You're not being proactive enough") or too general ("You guys always drop the ball") or emotionally charged ("This is unacceptable.")

The problem with feedback like this is that it feels more like criticism than guidance. It triggers our defenses, often leading us to dismiss it outright or react impulsively. But here's where we can tap into our emotional intelligence; when we resist the urge to react and instead focus on directing the feedback, we can uncover something valuable.

How to Turn Dirt into Seeds

Here's a simple process for handling messy feedback with poise and purpose:

1. Pause and Breathe

When feedback lands poorly, our first reaction might be emotional: anger, frustration, or embarrassment. We should try to recognize the trigger and give ourselves a moment. Taking a breath allows our emotional brain to settle so we can respond, not react.

2. Separate the Delivery from the Message

The delivery may feel careless or hurtful, but we shouldn't let that block us from hearing the message. We can ask ourselves: What is the core of what they're trying to say? Even if it's buried in frustration or poor wording, there's often a valid point from a different viewpoint.

3. Get Specifics

If the feedback is vague or generalized, we can take charge of the conversation and guide it toward clarity. We can ask for specific examples. To avoid making it sound like we're challenging, we may want to give a bit of context first.

We can ask:

"I want to make sure I understand your feedback. Could you help me understand what specifically you're referring to?"

"So that I know what needs adjusting, when you say 'this,' can you give me an example or a specific instance?"

This shifts the focus from blame to problem-solving, helping both parties zero in on the real issue.

4. Focus on the Solution

Once we've identified the specifics, we can redirect the conversation toward improvement. We can do this better by recruiting the feedback giver to brainstorm with us so we can create alignment in our understanding of the improvement.

Ask:

"What would a better outcome look like to you?"

Offer:

"Would it be helpful if I did X moving forward?"

This approach demonstrates our willingness to listen, engage, and act, turning a tense exchange into a productive discussion.

The delivery manager, despite feeling her frustration simmering under the surface, took a breath and resisted the urge to argue back. Instead, she calmly asked the project manager, "Can you tell me what specific issue you're seeing? Is there something my team can clarify or address?"

This simple question shifted the conversation. The project manager, caught off guard, paused and then explained: "There are errors in the expansions because your group didn't configure the parameters correctly."

Now, the problem was clear. The "You guys always do this" wasn't about everything—it was about one specific software configuration or product error. With that information, the delivery manager could address the real issue. She realized that when the product was expanded, the previous parameters were being used, causing glitches in the current project. She offered to get the support area involved to see what was causing the problem when the software was being updated. By holding off and guiding the conversation, she turned the messy feedback into a practical solution and strengthened trust in the process.

Messy feedback may feel like dirt at first, but it often contains seeds of insight, it's just a matter of discovering them. With a little emotional intelligence: pausing, listening, and directing the conversation, you can sift through the mess and find something valuable. This manager's story shows that even when feedback feels triggering, we can use it to grow and solve real problems.

Summary: The Knots that Trigger Defensiveness

Feedback is one of the most misunderstood tools in the workplace. Despite its potential to promote development, it's often avoided, mishandled, or delivered in ways that create tension rather than progress. Poorly delivered feedback, whether vague, overly critical, or misaligned with meaningful outcomes, leaves receivers feeling defensive or demoralized.

Another common issue is lack of recognition. Without specific and genuine acknowledgment, team members can feel unseen and undervalued, leading to disengagement and a lack of motivation. Similarly, when corrective feedback is delayed or avoided, small issues escalate into larger problems, eroding trust and creating a culture of frustration and high turnover.

Receiving feedback is its own challenge. Emotional triggers and poorly phrased critiques can make it difficult to extract value from the conversation. Instead of fostering growth, feedback often becomes a source of dread for both giver and receiver, creating missed opportunities for alignment and development.

Untangling the Knots

When approached with intention and care, feedback becomes a powerful tool for strengthening relationships and driving meaningful growth. Here's how to untangle the challenges and make feedback effective:

Provide Recognition with the CARE Model:

Recognition feedback reinforces positive behavior by being specific, clear, and meaningful. This framework ensures recognition is more than a vague "good job" and instead delivers praise that motivates and inspires. The CARE model offers three actionable steps:

Context & Action: Highlight the specific behavior or effort.

Result: Connect the action to a tangible outcome.

Effect: Explain its broader significance and value.

Deliver Corrective Feedback with the FRAME Model:

Corrective feedback requires clarity, empathy, and collaboration. This method ensures difficult conversations are constructive, focused, and aligned with shared goals. The FRAME model provides a structured approach:

Facts: Describe the situation objectively without blame.

Result: Explain the impact of behavior or action.

Align: Clarify the desired outcome or objective.

Map Solutions: Collaborate on actionable next steps.

Engage: Confirm understanding and commitment to progress.

Receive Feedback with Curiosity:

Effective feedback is a two-way street. To make the most of feedback received, manage emotional triggers, ask clarifying questions, and separate personal feelings from actionable insights. By listening with curiosity and reframing even poorly delivered feedback as an opportunity for growth, we can turn raw input into meaningful insight.

Through these frameworks, we can see how feedback, whether positive or corrective, should be approached with respect and a focus on partnership. In this way, effective feedback goes beyond addressing performance since it can also build confidence and align individuals with shared goals.

But what happens when the message is clear, but still misunderstood because the tone is misread, the silence misinterpreted, or it just lands differently than we intended? It may be a matter of culture, quietly shaping how we express ourselves or navigate disagreement. Let's look at how culture influences the way we communicate and why awareness is one of the most powerful tools a leader can develop.

To effectively communicate, we must realize that we are all different in the way we perceive the world.

— Tony Robbins

CHAPTER 4

Cross-Cultural Communication

Lessons from a Third Culture Kid

I got home from school one day to find my mother in a strangely excited and giddy mood.

"Maria! Guess what! Your father has been transferred. We're moving to Rome!"

I realized that the exuberance being displayed by my mother meant that life as I knew it was about to be upended.

I knew the decision had already been made, but I remember asking, "Do they have *Scooby Doo* cartoons there?" At least that would give me a sense of stability.

"Um. I'm sure they do!"

Within two months we had moved, and I became a Third Culture Kid. A "TCK" is someone who has lived in a different culture from that of their family during a significant part of their childhood[15].

My parents were the first wave of Cubans who thought they would return to Cuba in a few weeks after the Bay of Pigs invasion, but after that failed venture, they became Philadelphians, sucked up the cold weather, and never returned to Cuba again.

---

[15] David C. Pollock, Ruth E. Van Reken, and Michael V. Pollock. *Third Culture Kids: Growing Up Among Worlds*, 3rd ed, (Boston: Nicholas Brealey Publishing, 2017).

That first stint in Rome is full of wonderful memories. After the initial shock of finding that my mother had misled me, since there were no Scooby Doo cartoons on national Italian broadcasting channels, I was forced to play outside and figure out how to communicate with my Italian neighbor Claudia.

The next ten years saw us relocating a few more times. During the middle of my sophomore year, my dad announced we would be repatriating to Philadelphia. The stress of his job as financial director and the difficulties adapting to the culture in Mexico had given him health issues and he was done.

All in all, I attended seven schools and three universities, so, being the new kid became quite common for me. As nerve-racking as it was, I eventually got used to it and along with the anxiety came a little excitement, since every new adventure would bring with it the possibility of reinventing myself.

The constant change helped me learn to become adaptable. I also needed to learn to read people, since what was fun and cool in one place might not play over so well in another. They say Third Culture Kids learn leadership attributes from observing and learning, which makes them flexible and adaptable. My upbringing had an impact on my interests and career choices, and the skills I learned from all the traveling and assimilating turned out to be assets in my career.

Always the New Kid

Being the new kid at school every couple of years meant getting over the initial shyness that is natural when you feel at a disadvantage or put on the spot. It required getting out of my comfort zone constantly and mustering the courage to face my own vulnerability. At one point at the American school in Mexico City, I had to figure out what to do during recess. There was no cafeteria, merely outdoor tables and a canteen store to buy food.

A few times I tried hiding in the bathroom, but it was just too depressing. Even in my fourteen-year-old mind I realized that cowardly sitting in a bathroom for fear of social rejection was just not an option. Eventually, I noticed that right in front of the store, some cool kids would sit at a particular table and just hang out, flirt and joke around. I figured I would try to attach myself to them inconspicuously.

Some ignored me and others interacted with me, and all in all, the lunch period seemed to go well. Many of those kids had been in school together for years, but there was always turn over, as new expat kids came and went. I observed the dynamics of how the kids got along, what the rules of engagement were, what seemed appropriate and inappropriate in the banter. As time went by and I had figured it all out, my father would announce we were moving, and I had to start all over again.

What I learned and was reinforced over and over in my TCK experience was that in any environment, the power of observation and adaptation is key. It's not just about observing people, it's about figuring out the context in which they interact, as well as the underlying motivations and behaviors.

> In any environment, the power of observation and adaptation is key.

Let's dive into these TCK insights and see how they can provide lessons for our professional lives. Adapting to a new environment can feel like trying to find our way through a maze without a map.

In the workplace, professionals are constantly faced with market shifts that can feel just as daunting.

Here are a few of my Third Culture Kid lessons that can be applied to the workplace:

1. Get out of Your Comfort Zone

Even if it feels uncomfortable at times, it does us good to step out of our comfort zone to grow and succeed. This may involve taking on new projects, presenting ideas in meetings, or adapting to new roles. I was called upon to coach a new quality control director who needed to spend less time doing Gemba walks and more time becoming involved in higher level projects. We love what we know and what's comfortable, but life isn't static and with new environments come new opportunities.

When we embrace discomfort as a sign of growth, it's often a signal that we're on the brink of something new and challenging. For the QC director, the shift from hands-on work to strategic involvement may have seemed uncomfortable initially, but it was an opportunity for her to open avenues for leadership development and greater influence in the organization.

Stepping out of our comfort zone doesn't always mean making immediate drastic changes but it does mean taking a deep breath and doing something we might not normally do. We can challenge ourselves or our teams to take on a new responsibility, initiate a new process, or seek feedback on a project. Over time, these actions build on each other, leading to significant personal and professional growth.

Another lesson I learned was to reframe challenges as opportunities. Every time my dad would say "We're moving to….", it would cause a knot in my stomach. Change does that to people; it's inevitable. The fear of the unknown is probably ingrained in our DNA to protect us, but once that initial discomfort wore off, it was easier to see the opportunities hiding behind the challenge. I could strategically and deliberately reinvent my new persona at my new location.

The QC director may have felt a twinge of nervousness at abandoning her familiar and successful routine but reframing the challenge as an opportunity helped her develop new skills and made a broader impact as she reinvented herself in the process. She also admitted that there was a certain excitement that came with embracing her new position and the power and responsibilities that came with it.

Each time we push beyond our comfort zone, we build resilience and adaptability, which are essential for forward momentum. These experiences prepare us for future challenges and make it easier to navigate uncertainty in our career journey.

2. Avoid the Silo

In those first moments of discomfort at my new school, I tried to avoid the situation by hiding out. I realized that it made me feel even more disconnected and unhappy, as I knew life was happening without me.

When we avoid engaging with others, we often miss out on valuable experiences, learning opportunities and connections. In a corporate setting, isolation may show up in the form of a silo mentality and can be a barrier to growth. It's easier to retreat into familiar routines, or think only about our immediate surroundings or KPI's, but that can limit our exposure to new ideas or opportunities.

Just like my school experience, where I eventually realized I needed to step out and engage with my peers, in a corporate environment, avoiding interaction can lead to missed opportunities for networking or making important improvements.

For instance, one sales director I coached made it a point to regularly step out of his comfort zone by inviting high-level stakeholders, such as the international director, to business reviews on performance, market access and opportunities. This wasn't required, nor was it an easy move, and most people would feel uneasy exposing their numbers and practices to higher-level scrutiny. However, the rewards far outweighed the initial discomfort.

Turns out, the sales director's bold move increased his visibility within the company and also opened doors for his team members. By inviting review and fostering open discussions he created an environment of transparency and continuous improvement. The willingness to expose himself and his team to potential criticism strengthened their reputation, brought in new ideas for growth, and promoted transparency and goodwill among different areas.

Avoiding isolation also means actively seeking out relationships beyond our immediate circle. In the workplace, this could involve reaching out to colleagues in different departments, attending cross-functional meetings, or participating in company-wide initiatives. These interactions can foster unexpected collaborations. The sales director's example shows that building relationships with higher-ups or those in different areas of the business can lead to increased opportunities for everyone involved.

For leaders, it's important to create a culture where engagement is encouraged and rewarded. This could involve organizing team-building activities or simply recognizing and rewarding those who take the initiative to connect with others.

It's worth noting that when we avoid silos and actively engage with others, the benefits often extend beyond our immediate experience. As a TCK in a new environment, my decision to sit with the cool kids, despite the risk of rejection, paid off in giving me the social recognition I craved.

The sales director's decision to invite senior stakeholders into his review despite the risk of being scrutinized or criticized not only enhanced his own career but also provided his team with greater exposure and opened opportunities for innovation. This ripple effect of engagement can lead to a more connected, motivated and successful team overall.

3. Observe Dynamics and Rules of Engagement

One of the most important lessons I've learned from my TCK experience is the ability to pick up on the cues that exist in different groups and adapt accordingly. There's always context and unwritten subtext that we can miss if we're not paying attention.

In a corporate environment, we may find ourselves in the middle of a merger, suddenly managing a new team, or transitioning to a new company. Each of these shifts brings its own set of cultural norms, unspoken expectations, and underlying power dynamics.

Much like stepping into new schools as I had to as a child, we may have to walk into an existing system where relationships, status, and behaviors have already been established. Despite what we may assume, the real rules of engagement are embedded in the company culture and day-to-day interactions.

We may need to observe who speaks up in meetings, or whose opinion carries weight even if they aren't in the room.[16] How is conflict managed? What nuances are there and how can we figure out how to navigate them? Learning to read the room is essential for adapting our style and navigating the cultural landscape more effectively. The ability to observe and adapt can make the difference between struggling and thriving.

Navigating Corporate Culture

Years ago, I was working on a customer service training initiative with the former Nokia Siemens Networks, a joint venture created to capitalize on growing demand for mobile broadband and network services in the late aughts. Even a few years into the venture, the struggle to reconcile cultural differences persisted, rooted in distinct ways of working.

Siemens, a German company, I was told, was characterized by a somewhat hierarchical environment where decision-making processes were deliberate and methodical, with a tendency toward risk-aversion. On the other hand, Nokia, the Finnish company, embodied a more informal culture with a flatter organizational structure that promoted quicker decision-making and innovation.

---

[16] Mike Ashie, "Cracking the Code: How Observing Workplace Dynamics Can Set You Up for Success," *Mike Ashie* (blog), June 7, 2023.

The merger of these two distinct corporate cultures presented several challenges in operations. For example, when it came to decision-making, Siemens's structured approach often slowed down decision-making, a contrast to Nokia's more fast-paced style. This led to internal disconnects and delays, especially in the rapidly evolving telecommunications industry.

When it came to management styles, the top-down hierarchical culture of Siemens was often at odds with Nokia's flatter, more collaborative approach, creating friction between management teams and confusion among employees over expected behaviors and practices.

Nokia's push for innovation and flexibility, combined with Siemens' emphasis on process adherence and risk management, led to further struggles as the joint venture failed to adapt quickly to market changes. The two distinct corporate cultures seemed incapable of integrating, leading to a lack of a united front, both internally and externally. Among other things, this lack of cohesion contributed to operational inefficiencies and ultimately impacted the venture's performance.

This textbook example is what management expert Peter Drucker meant when he said that "Culture eats strategy for breakfast," highlighting the overpowering influence of culture on organizational success.

Had there been a more deliberate focus on observation and cultural due diligence before the merger, or establishing common ground, a different outcome could have emerged. Conducting a deeper cultural assessment, understanding strengths and weaknesses of each company's cultural framework, and planning for the gaps could have bridged these differences, fostering a more unified leadership vision.

Navigating different cultures around the globe, and understanding corporate culture requires the same skills: observation and adaptation. When we step into a new workplace or team, it's kind of like entering a whole new country, where the rules may be different from what we're used to. Each company has its own vibe, values and unwritten rules that can make or break our experience there. Just as we pay attention to social cues in an intercultural setting, being attuned to the nuances of our corporate environment is key for success.

Our Cultural Lens

One summer, while visiting my family in Philadelphia as I usually did with my two children since we lived in Mexico, my good friend Jim came by to pick me up at my sister's house to have lunch. I introduced him to my daughter Lorena who was around twelve at the time. I looked away momentarily and heard a nervous laugh but didn't think much of it. When we were at the restaurant, Jim said "I think Lorena really liked me." "Really?" I asked. "Yes," he affirmed. "She gave me a big hug."

Fast forward a few hours later: I was with Lorena, who seemed anxious. "Oh, Mom, how embarrassing with your friend!" she exclaimed. I asked, "What are you talking about, sweetheart?"

She explained:

"I approached him to greet him with a kiss, but he instinctively moved backward, and I was going to fall forward, so I grabbed him by the neck!"

I let out a huge chuckle.

"What? Oh, no, did he say anything? How embarrassing!"

Tweens are embarrassed about most things, but I told her that he had interpreted it as an effusive gesture of affection—and why not let him hold on to that belief? We both knew that this had been a case of a cultural mismatch.

Anyone who has visited or worked abroad knows that the first greeting is a tough one, since most people don't know whether they should kiss—once, twice or more? Do you hug, shake hands, bow or just say hello? It's especially challenging if you're trying to make a good first impression but the social rules haven't been established yet.

When we think about culture, much comes to mind: traditions, food, customs, beliefs, norms and a host of other things. My favorite definition of culture is Geert Hofstede's tried and true: "Culture is the collective programing of the mind that distinguishes one group from another."[17] It's simple and clean, and in that context, highlights our alignment of thought, which is conducive to the behaviors and affinities that we usually associate with other cultural elements. It's the way we do things, the rules of the game, what's okay and not okay, what we prefer.

Thinking about culture in this way lets us see how layered we are. Culture is something we learn and share, not something we're born with. Understanding culture in this way helps us see why these differences matter, especially in a globalized world where cross-cultural interactions are more common than ever. This

---

[17] Geert Hofstede, *Cultures and Organizations: Software of the Mind*, (New York: McGraw-Hill, 1991).

understanding is important in both personal and professional relationships.

The iceberg analogy shown below is commonly used to explain culture in education. Using "the iceberg," people can more easily visualize the distinction between things that are easily identified and perceivable (above the surface) versus those less obvious and subtle (below the surface). Usually, we perceive things above the surface such as food, environment, dress, race, infrastructure, language, music, etc. with our five senses.

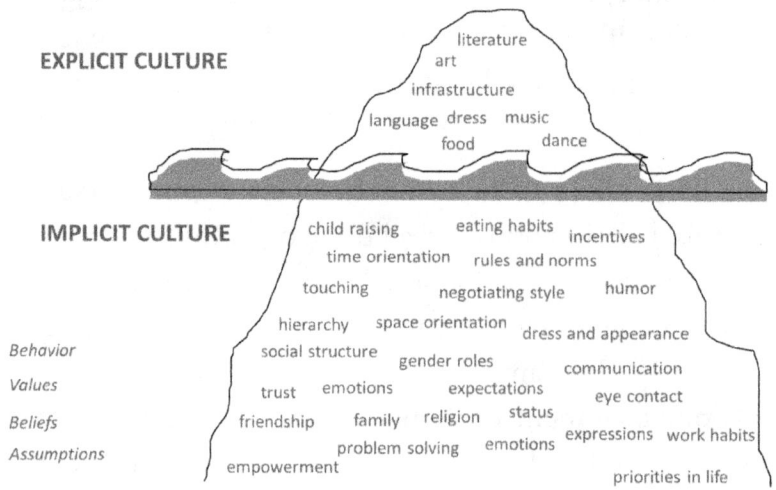

It gets a little trickier when we look beneath the surface. At that level, the dynamics between people become more complex, as they start to involve values, beliefs, and behaviors. Examples include communication styles, perception of time, relationships, friendship, family, hierarchy, risk-taking, education, gender roles, and child-raising, to name a few.

You'll notice these elements are perceived in different ways, depending on the culture. That's for a very specific reason, which requires context, deeper understanding and of course, time. Just like the iceberg, the obvious aspects of culture, such as language and dress, are easy to spot. It's the hidden values and beliefs that often trip us up in intercultural interactions. For managers leading multicultural teams, failing to recognize these underlying differences can lead to miscommunication and conflict.

While in our native culture, we rarely notice our surroundings, like fish swimming effortlessly in water. But once we step outside our familiar environment, new ways of doing things and different expectations that come with them may feel strange or unfamiliar. This is when we start questioning and comparing, which is a natural response as our minds try to make sense of the differences and fit them into familiar categories. Suddenly, we feel like a fish out of water—floundering, disoriented, and longing for the comfort of what we know.

Not everyone must relocate to a new environment, but many of us experience cross-cultural work dynamics, as businesses have expanded globally and many functional teams have become virtual teams. Navigating the intricacies of multi-cultural teams can be challenging, as we are faced with behaviors that puzzle or irritate us.

As a cross-cultural trainer, I've spent years preparing executives for foreign assignments and heard plenty of familiar complaints once they settled in like what my father said when he moved to Mexico decades ago. Like him, the leaders were often blindsided by how much cultural nuance affects communication.

It's helpful to realize what our values are and what makes us tick before applying our methods to others. Socrates was wise when he said, "Know thyself." That's one of the reasons I start all my learning sessions with a self-assessment. The first step in cultivating cultural intelligence is figuring out our starting point. Some of the questions I include are:

- What values did you learn when you were young?
- What's important to you?
- How does that affect your interactions with others?
- What do you expect from other people in a social or work setting?
- How do you deal with conflict?
- How do you promote cooperation?

These types of questions help us realize that we are not a blank slate; rather, we carry a host of preferences and tendencies, which naturally will affect us when judging other people or situations.

I usually give my students or clients a yellow-tinted, semi-transparent plastic sheet, which represents the lens through which they view the world. I will also typically hold up a blue one. When they look through their lens at me, they realize how perspectives change. The thing is, we can't just shed our whole programming, including values, preferences, and affinities, but we can exercise awareness and realize that though we will never see the world through the other colored lens, we can superimpose one over the other to get a nice shade of green, just by understanding the context of the other person's environment and culture through natural curiosity and due diligence.

Gone are the days when cross-cultural interaction was an exception in a mostly homogeneous workplace. Today, many of us collaborate daily with teams scattered across the globe. These interactions are no longer rare, which makes it all the more important to recognize how our cultural filters shape the way we communicate.

Figuring out how to communicate with people who have a completely different perspective or culture can be a bit unnerving. My experience working with leaders and teams always takes us to the same place; how to communicate to really connect and collaborate. When elements are involved that cause noise (and, of course, I mean this mostly in a figurative way), that connection becomes affected and can get lost. Cultural noise is very powerful and can cause a huge disconnect between people.

A few years ago, I was brought in for training at a Spanish bank with employees from both Spain and nearly every Latin American country, since most of the business was conducted in Spanish. During a cross-cultural session, I found it amusing that the most intense complaints didn't just come from differences with the Spaniards, but also from Latin Americans themselves, frustrated with each other's varying levels of courtesy, responsiveness, and communication style.

The most common complaint I heard dealt with greeting protocols. Usually, they came from Mexicans or Central Americans, who felt that Caribbeans or some South Americans were rude because they didn't greet them properly.

I had seen a similar pattern at a large spirits company in Mexico. Because everyone spoke Spanish, the assumption was that they shared not just a language, but the same unspoken rules. That assumption raised expectations and amplified the friction, because when differences cropped up, they were judged as a personal rather than a cultural issue. Those assumptions would not have been made had the other person been from a less familiar country.

We often operate with cultural blind spots, unaware of the gaps in our understanding until something goes wrong. Johari's Window, a psychological tool developed by Joseph Luft and Harry Ingham, divides our awareness into four quadrants: what is known to us and others, what is known to us but not to others, what is known to others and not us, and what is unknown to both parties. In cross-cultural settings, the "unknown unknowns" can cause friction because neither side realizes they are operating with different cultural assumptions.

To illustrate, while writing my final project paper on cross-cultural management styles for my master's program, I decided to interview Cuban managers who were expats working in Mexico and their Mexican team members or counterparts. It amused me to discover that while the Cubans thought that they had mostly been successful in their communications with their teams, the Mexicans confided in me that they had felt offended by the Cubans' aggressive style and tone on many occasions. One Cuban manager even admitted that he had inadvertently made one of his staff members cry a couple of times due to the way he gave feedback, which surprised him and made him realize there was a disconnect in their styles.

Communicating in a Cross-Cultural Environment

One story that has stayed with me for years came from "Pedro," a Mexican auto executive whom I was preparing for an expat assignment. He was on a business trip in Detroit and had an urgent situation that required a sign-off from an American colleague. He went to Owen's office and saw that he was on the phone. He tried to make eye contact, but seeing that Owen was engrossed in his conversation, Pedro walked into his office and waved to get his attention.

Obviously annoyed, Owen stopped his phone conversation, looked up at Pedro and asked, "Can't you see I'm on the phone?" When Pedro tried to explain the urgent situation, Owen cut him off and said, "When I'm done, I'll look into it." and did the unthinkable. He turned his back to Pedro. As Pedro told me this story, I could hear the indignation in his voice as he re-lived the experience, feeling the humiliation of Owen's apparent disdain. He told me that after that experience, he wrote off Owen and made sure to avoid him at all costs.

Although in Pedro's mind, this conflict felt very personal, walking him through the cultural elements helped him see something he hadn't before, which thankfully brought him some peace about his interaction with Owen. One of the elements measured in many intercultural tools is whether a culture is more relationship-oriented or task-oriented, as highlighted by Fons Trompenaars and Charles Hampden-Turner in *Riding the Waves of Culture.*

As Pedro confirmed on the cultural assessment he completed, he was very relationship-oriented, so his expectation was that Owen would show solidarity and give priority to his presence. In Mexico, relationships are highly valued, making the greeting protocol and other displays of courtesy very important.

When people converse in a group in Mexico, great care is taken to avoid turning one's back on others, to ensure inclusiveness and respect. Failing to do so can be perceived as an act of disdain or contempt. Protecting others' dignity and helping them save face is a fundamental aspect of social interaction.

In the US, however, people tend to be more task-oriented, which was probably the case with Owen. That usually involves doing things in a sequential way, prioritizing them on a first-come, first-served basis. Time and space are valued and guarded as part of one's personal patrimony, and interruptions are considered rude and imposing.

Owen probably felt that Pedro's approach was aggressive and selfish and thus, took a defensive approach by blocking further engagement with him. It was, I explained to Pedro, as if he had reached into Owen's pocket, pulled out his wallet and taken money without his consent. He probably felt a bit violated.

Pedro's perspective suddenly changed. He had seen the situation from his cultural filter and never considered the narrative from Owen's point of view. We don't know what we don't know, but that's precisely what makes it crucial to avoid jumping to conclusions when it comes to assumptions regarding the intentions in our interactions.

Bridging the Gaps

When we find ourselves amid a cultural disconnect, it can feel frustrating, confusing and even personal. But recognizing that these moments often stem from differing cultural values, rather than intentional rudeness, can be the first step toward bridging the gap. Here are some strategies that can help navigate these situations:

Cultivate Cultural Awareness: We can start by educating ourselves about the cultural norms and values of the people we interact with regularly. Two good books are *"The Culture Map"* by Erin Meyer and *"Kiss, Bow or Shake Hands"*, by Terri Morrison and Wayne A. Conaway. Whether it's our colleagues, clients or even service providers from other regions, understanding their cultural background can prevent misunderstandings before they arise.

One project manager opened a map when speaking to colleagues in India and asked where they were located and what their city or town was known for so he could visualize them better in his mind. He shared a little tidbit of his own as well. Every interaction for him became an opportunity to broaden his cultural knowledge and connect with his colleagues at a deeper level.

I like to learn greetings in other people's languages and then delight when they smile and greet me back. It seems a pleasant surprise to them, since it shows that I took the time and interest and it creates a sense of goodwill and connection. It's a simple way to build an initial rapport and encourage further questions and sharing. I sometimes ask for a few additional words, repeat them back, and get feedback on my pronunciation.

Ask, Don't Assume: Showing natural curiosity when it comes to new cultures can help establish the understanding that we are navigating unknown territory. For example, if colleagues are celebrating a national holiday, asking about the origin of the holiday shows that we are eager to learn. It's always flattering when someone shows a natural curiosity toward us, and it's nice to share.

When working with new cross-cultural teams, we can either ignore the cultural element and let it come back and bite us later, or we can face it head on. I recommend recognizing it from the very beginning to lessen the storming[18] phase of team development, the stage where everyone is trying to figure out the rules of the game. If leading a new intercultural team, starting with a team-building activity in which team members share a bit about themselves, their cultures, and how they prefer to work can be a great way to kick off a new project.

There are different ways to conduct this exercise, from an informal conversation to a more structured debrief following a questionnaire that may include questions about one's culture, preferred methods of communication or strategies for managing conflict. See Appendix B: New Team Alignment Blueprint for ideas.

When sensing tension or confusion in an interaction, we can consider asking clarifying questions rather than making assumptions. Simple inquiries such as, "Am I greeting you correctly?" can open the door to better understanding.

State Your Intent and Assume Positive Intent in Others: It's easy to assume. That's why it can really help when we give people a bit of context of what's going in. We can let our new team know we have good intentions and want to have a good working relationship.

Too often, we hear about people getting caught up in perceived offenses because someone used an outdated term or made a comment or observation that seemed ignorant. I have heard my share of ignorant comments, but rather than get angry, it's better to embrace the moment as a teaching opportunity. None of us are experts in every cultural nuance or practice, so it would behoove us

---

[18] Bruce W. Tuckman, "Developmental Sequence in Small Groups," *Psychological Bulletin 63*, no. 6 (1965).

to show grace to others as we would hope to receive if we made a mistake.

For example, when people say to me "Your parents are Cuban? You don't look Cuban." I take the opportunity to educate, rather than berate the person for a perceived "microaggression." I might share the fact that Cuba has a rich and diverse ethnic population and was one of the last Spanish colonies and had a large and constant Spanish influx.

I admit being just as surprised when a colleague whom I thought was Indian, told me she was from Trinidad and Tobago. When I asked her about that, she kindly explained that a large Indian diaspora from Northern India settled in the Caribbean in the nineteenth century. I'm glad she wasn't offended by my ignorance. The way I see it, there's always an opportunity to act as an ambassador and bestow the gift of knowledge.

When someone behaves in a way that we may consider rude, it's a good moment to ask ourselves whether the issue may be cultural. If the answer is yes, we have made the most important shift in our thinking, by being empathetic and admitting the possibility that the behavior may have been completely logical or consistent from the other person's perspective. This shift in perspective can soften our response. Giving each other the benefit of the doubt can elicit a more positive response all around.

Use the Disclaimer Method: I learned this one the hard way. When I lived in Mexico, I had a gardener. I asked him to prune the trees and mow the lawn. When he let the bushes and trees grow too much, in my frustration and attempt to give him feedback I said something like, "Jaime, mowing the lawn is something I can do myself. I need you to prune the trees." After that he never came back.

Though I thought it was no big deal, I remembered my father's lament about Mexican sensibilities. I realized that my feedback style had been too direct, and that Jaime had felt humiliated, since I had implied that his work was of little value.

With the next gardener, I decided to use what I call the "disclaimer method". I told him that I was American and tended to be direct to the point of sounding blunt, but to please not take it personally and let me know if something seemed off. Though we had our differences of opinion, we were able to communicate without him giving up like the first guy.

This "disclaimer" method can help us address the cultural elephant in the room from the very beginning and acknowledge that cultural noise may make interactions a bit more difficult. This makes it easier to establish goodwill, encouraging others to share when they feel uncomfortable or misunderstood. By creating a space where feedback is welcomed, everyone can navigate cultural differences more effectively.

Reflect and Adjust: After a cultural disconnect, we should take time to reflect on what happened and what we could do differently next time. This self-awareness helps improve future interactions when we make a mistake. The ability to bounce back from a disconnect is a key element in emotional intelligence.

I vividly recall one instance when I had to learn this myself. I was asked to provide a virtual keynote to women in a Mexican company for International Women's Day. I put together typical female archetypes and included one for women who are perceived as strong in their styles and labeled it "the bitch". Today the word is not taboo in the US, and I had seen references to this archetype in various TEDx talks, but it came across as harsh and vulgar in my presentation in Spanish for the Mexican group.

After the session, I received negative feedback on that point and initially felt dejected, realizing I had miscalculated my audience's reaction, but reflected and learned. Though I had lived in Mexico for twenty years, there were still things I didn't know. I apologized to one of the stakeholders, admitting I had made assumptions and thanked them for their feedback. Rather than stew or give up and avoid similar situations, I welcomed the opportunity to learn yet another new thing about a culture that I thought I knew so well. Live and learn.

Cultural differences will inevitably show up in interactions in our ever-shrinking world. But the real challenge isn't in the differences themselves, but in how we choose to respond to them. By approaching each interaction with humility and a genuine desire to learn, we can bridge cultural gaps and enrich our own experience of the world. Let's take a look at some cultural patterns in communication.

Low-Context Communication

I was conducting a cross-cultural workshop for a company in the auto industry that had teams working both in Mexico and the US. One of the American participants asked me, "Why is it that my Mexican counterparts contact me via interoffice chat and write something like, '*Hi, Sam, how are you?*'— and then silence! They don't tell me what they need until I respond." He was frustrated because for him, this was a waste of time; he didn't see the point of engaging in small talk if there was something that needed to be done.

Remember the relationship vs. task thing? Well, this is a classic example. In my experience, of all the cultural dimensions identified by respected interculturalists and sociologists regarding such dynamics as approaches to time, risk-taking, locus of control, hierarchy, and more, what inevitably crops up as the most pertinent and challenging is communication. As the main vehicle for interaction, it stands to reason that this dimension is essential in engaging effectively with others, but not everyone goes by the same rules.

Even if you eliminated all the obvious barriers such as language and accents, so many other invisible and inaudible barriers can still get in the way of a successful interaction. Effective cross-cultural communication requires not only awareness of differences in styles but also an understanding of how to bridge those styles for increased mutual understanding.

Sam, the American participant, was more task-driven. He saw the team's primary goal as completing the job as efficiently as possible. Taking time to ask team members how they were doing or pausing for small talk felt counterproductive to him. In his view, communication had a clear purpose: to convey information. He believed it was the sender's responsibility to deliver the message succinctly and directly, minimizing the need for interpretation by the receiver. This task and objective oriented approach aligns with what we call a low-context, direct communication style in the intercultural world.

In low-context cultures such as the U.S., clarity and efficiency are highly valued. The expectation is that information is explicit and self-contained within the words themselves, the less ambiguity, the better. For someone like Sam, communication serves a functional purpose: to get to the point and move the task forward.

Countries such as the U.S., Germany, and those in Scandinavia favor a direct, explicit, and task-focused communication style, rooted in cultural values of individualism and efficiency. The assumption is that people communicate primarily to exchange specific information and that words should carry the full weight of the message. Ambiguous messages that require interpretation are seen as risky, since they may foster misunderstanding; so, the goal is to be as clear and straightforward as possible.

This preference for directness is also tied to a historical reliance on formal systems and institutions that support task completion. When systems function reliably, people are less dependent on personal relationships to get things done. As a result, small talk and interpersonal bonding are often seen as secondary to the task, or even as a waste of time.

In these cultures, the ideal interaction is one in which the information stands on its own. Silence, hesitation, or vagueness can create discomfort because they suggest something is being left unsaid or that the task is being delayed. That's why, for someone such as Sam, skipping the pleasantries and getting straight to the point feels like a sign of respect—both for efficiency and for the other person's time.

I worked with another leader from the U.S. who was leading a team from Mexico and found himself frustrated because members of his team would hesitate to give him bad news. When they finally would, he felt like they were beating around the bush, and it took significant effort to extract the point. For someone like him, who was used to a low-context communication style, this felt incredibly aggravating. He wanted straightforward answers and instead, received information that, to him, seemed wrapped in layers of explanations, caveats, and excuses.

This is a common experience for low-context communicators when working with teams from high-context cultures. They expect communication to be efficient and unambiguous, yet the message they receive often seems to require extensive interpretation. In his case, the intent of his team members wasn't to withhold information or shift blame but rather to avoid causing him distress. For them, delivering bad news indirectly was a way of softening the impact and minimizing potential conflict. What he saw as inefficiency, they saw as an attempt to preserve harmony and avoid unnecessary emotional discomfort.

High-Context Communication

To understand the dynamics that took place between Sam and his counterpart, it's important to recognize the patterns of high-context communication. High-context cultures, such as Mexico, Japan, and many Middle Eastern countries, place a much greater emphasis on the unspoken elements of communication. In these cultures, people often rely on shared understandings and subtle exchanges to convey meaning. Much of the message is communicated through tone, body language, and the broader context of the interaction and personal history, rather than words.

This style reflects a deeper cultural value on collectivism and social harmony. Historically, in many high-context societies, institutions weren't always seen as reliable, so people learned to depend heavily on personal networks and relationships. Trust and relationships were (and often still are) the foundation for getting things done.

A clear example of this in Mexico is the *"tanda,"* an informal banking system in which neighbors, friends, or colleagues agree to contribute a set monetary amount weekly into a collective pot. Participants take turns receiving the full sum, based on the number of participants and the order determined when the *tanda,* starts. For those who get their pay-out early, it's like a loan, while those who receive it later use it as a savings method.

The system relies entirely on trust since everyone must keep their commitment to contribute weekly, with no formal contracts involved. This practice highlights how, in a high-context culture, relationships and mutual reliance replace institutional safeguards.

Just as trust forms the backbone of systems such as the *tanda*, it also plays a key role in everyday communication. In Sam's case, he realized that for his Mexican counterparts, the need to maintain and nurture relationships through communication was just as important as ensuring the task was completed. In a relationship-oriented culture such as Mexico, things flow more effectively when care is taken to preserve dignity and avoid conflict.

Also, in Mexico, it's essential to go through the proper protocol of greeting people respectfully, whether in person, over chat, or on video calls. Skipping over the courtesies can come across as disdainful. Jumping too quickly into making a request without breaking the ice can feel selfish or demanding, causing offense.

I once rushed into the office, distracted and focused on picking up a document left there for me. Without thinking, I quickly asked the administrative assistant, Dulce, for the file without having properly greeted her first.

Dulce interlaced her fingers, gave me a cold look, and said, "Buenos días, Maria," making no other movement. I immediately realized I had offended her by missing this important step. I had to pause, apologize for my rudeness, feebly explaining that I was distracted, and then greeted her properly with a kiss on the cheek. Only then did she smile and say, "Oh, it's fine," and handed over the document.

That small interaction reinforced how deeply ingrained these rituals of politeness and connection are. Without them, everyday tasks can become strained. In a relationship-oriented culture, establishing goodwill through proper greetings and respect is necessary to move things forward.

Once Sam understood this, a light bulb turned on in his head. He realized that something that he initially saw as an annoying habit on the part of his colleagues had a whole underlying reason. He decided it was worth it to take a little extra time to engage in small talk with his Mexican colleagues before diving into tasks. He now knew he was investing in building goodwill and trust within the team.

When we talked about this in the program, some of the Mexican participants smiled at my explanation, not realizing that a few of their American counterparts grew annoyed with their courtesy protocol. For them it was simply good manners to connect at a personal level first, and then patiently wait for implicit permission to make their request. It's awesome when people can finally interpret the values behind the behavior that, until that moment, had seemed confusing.

The shift in perspective is often the first step toward building more effective cross-cultural relationships. Once we understand the reasons behind different behaviors or communication styles, we can adapt and find common ground. Whether you tend to communicate in a more direct, low-context way or prefer a relationship-focused, high-context approach, learning to bridge these styles is very important for team collaboration.

You can reflect on your own cultural communication preferences by taking the quiz in Appendix C: Cultural Snapshots. It will help you assess where you fall on the high-context to low-context spectrum and adjust your interactions across cultures.

Summary: The Knots of that Distort Meaning

In a globalized world, the diversity of communication styles, cultural norms, and interpersonal expectations often leads to misunderstandings and friction in both personal and professional contexts. Challenges are compounded by a lack of awareness or preparation when navigating unfamiliar environments.

Another hurdle involves human nature, the natural discomfort that comes with stepping into the unknown. When we are joining a new team, managing cultural diversity, or adapting to unfamiliar norms, initial anxiety can make it tempting to resist change or retreat into old habits. Without reframing this discomfort as a chance to grow, we risk missing opportunities for connection and innovation.

Finally, communication styles vary widely across cultures. High-context communication values subtlety, relationships, and shared understanding, while low-context communication prioritizes directness and clarity. Misunderstandings often arise when these styles clash, creating unnecessary friction and misinterpretation.

Untangling the Knots

To navigate these challenges, three key strategies can help:

Cultivate Observation Skills: We should take time to observe before acting, learn to read verbal and nonverbal cues, and align our approach with the dynamics of the environment. Observation fosters understanding, while adaptability ensures our actions resonate with those around us.

Reframe Discomfort as Growth: We can view moments of uncertainty or change as opportunities rather than obstacles. Whether introducing ourselves to a new group or adapting to a different norm, stepping outside our comfort zone creates the space for personal development, stronger relationships, and innovation.

Bridge Communication Styles: We should recognize the differences between high-context and low-context communication. We can also practice cultural intelligence by observing, asking thoughtful questions, and assuming positive intent. By building awareness and adjusting our style, we can minimize misunderstandings.

Culture plays a huge role in shaping how we communicate. It influences everything, from how we give feedback to how we manage disagreement or show respect. Yet even when we understand our habits and those of others, communication can still get tangled.

And speaking of culture, every generation has its own culture and way of doing things. As we saw earlier on, technology has had an impact on many of our habits. When we pair generational and technological shifts, we find that communication patterns are bound to be affected as well.

Technology is not in itself the enemy. The enemy is using it to replace connection rather than deepen it.

— **Sherry Turkle**

CHAPTER 5

Generations, Technology, and Communication

―――――――⵿―――――――

The Death of the Phone Call

I had just called my daughter to clarify something we had been texting about, and she didn't pick up. A short moment later, she sent me a message: "I'm eating lunch. Just text me." -*Okay*, I thought, *so let me get this straight. She just used both hands to pick up the phone and write me that text, but she couldn't use one finger to press a button and put me on speaker mode and talk to me while she ate?* I was indignant. And, as I soon discovered, I wasn't the only parent having frustrating moments with their offspring on preferred methods of communication.

Ironically, my daughter would get just as annoyed when I wouldn't immediately answer a text. Due to the overwhelming number of dings and pings, I mute all notifications on my cell phone, with only the phone ringer enabled. I check messages in my own sweet time, much to the annoyance of some of my friends and family members who never let go of their devices, not even during trips to the bathroom.

After a few heated exchanges, we realized that our mutual frustration had to do with a difference in what

> Our concept of proper communication protocol may vary, depending on our age and experiences.

we considered the "right" way to communicate and what constituted proper protocol. The problem is that our concept of proper communication protocol may vary immensely from others, depending on our age and experience. We finally reached an agreement: If something required a response right away, she would just call me. Otherwise, we would simply text. I don't take rejected calls so personally anymore; I just leave a voice note, because voice mail is so last century.

Looking back at our modes of communication throughout history, for hundreds of years, people either visited in person or wrote a letter and patiently waited for a response. Around the beginning of the twentieth century, people gained the ability to call each other on the telephone. Since it was connected to the wall and the line was shared, callers had to go through the protocol of greeting and identifying themselves with whoever answered before talking to the desired party or leaving a message.

It afforded little privacy, usually involving a loud announcement of the caller's identity, which often led to questions and speculation. The caller had to brace themselves and be ready to make polite small talk with the "filters" before getting to the person they had called. Everyone had to learn to think on their feet and operate outside their comfort zone.

Screening calls didn't become a thing until caller ID took root in the late eighties and then people could delegate the message-taking to the answering machines when they didn't want to deal with a call or caller at that moment. Sometime around the nineties and aughts, beepers and radios became popular, and eventually cell phones went mainstream. This was the beginning of the end of landlines as people were able to connect with their desired party directly without filters. No more small talk with mothers, siblings, assistants, or any other person other than their desired party. Blessed freedom!

Texting was soon introduced as a feature, enabling people to send discreet messages instead of calling. This made communication so much more convenient and intimate, as we were guaranteed that the person we wanted to communicate with got the message without any intermediaries or noise. It was for their eyes only and could be read at the receiver's convenience, making it more discreet and direct.

However, with this greater autonomy made possible through asynchronous messaging, came the loss of an important interpersonal skill. It was no longer necessary to break the ice, make small talk or think on our feet; rather, we had the luxury of mulling over a response, getting external input or even crowdsourcing before sending out a witty reply. This may have had its advantages, but for the generations who came of age with this asynchronous technology, mostly Millennials and Gen Z, phone calls became outdated and irrelevant, just like vinyl records and rotary phones.

The downside of texting is that it created a strong aversion to having to deal with anything that might still require a phone call. When my daughter had an administrative issue with her university's student loan office, I told her to just call, but the idea of speaking to a stranger to solve an issue like that took her too far out of her comfort zone. She decided instead to take half a day off work to deal with the issue in person, even going so far as to wait an hour to be seen.

How much did that aversion cost her? Doing the math, she lost 4 hours of wages, spent money on gasoline, and wasted precious time waiting for help with a situation that could have been solved by a fifteen-minute call at most. Now we are beginning to see how this issue contributes to the loss of time and resources mentioned earlier in the Harris Poll.

Lest it seem like I'm trashing my daughter with all these anecdotes, I just want to point out that this attitude has become commonplace in our society, first among Millennials and now Gen Z, since the technology meant to make life more convenient stripped many of the skills needed to create rapport with strangers in real time without the benefit of non-verbal cues.

Phone phobia[19] is real, and I've seen it across cultures. It has contaminated the older generations too. Even in our private lives, we must now make appointments to make a phone call. If you call out of the blue and are not dying, you will hear the indignation in the receiver's voice. Cell phones are hardly used as phones anymore.

One of my clients had a young business development professional team member who met a potential client at a conference. The person she met seemed interested in her product. However, her later follow-up emails went unanswered. She was torn as to whether she should use the company phone number to call her contact. My question to her was: Why on earth not? What would she have to lose? Her potential client may have gotten lost in a swamp of emails. This is a good example of when you may need to reach into your toolbox and decide what method to use.

---

[19] John Dias, "Gen Z Developing Fear of Phone Calls, or 'Phone Phobia,'" *CBS News* New York, August 1, 2023

A study in Australia[20] showed that while 98 percent of Gen Z respondents agreed that it's important to stay connected with family and friends, the preferred modes are face-to-face or texting, with half of them saying that speaking on the phone makes them anxious. A whopping 60 percent of respondents said that they dreaded making or accepting a phone call, even when necessary, and four in ten admitted to "ghosting" (aka avoiding) someone to avoid a tough conversation. It turns out, phone coaches are now a thing—and they charge upwards of $500 an hour to teach people how to talk on the phone.

Ghosts in the Office

And speaking of ghosting—the act of disappearing without explanation—it seems that this regrettable habit has seeped from dating culture into professional environments, and the damage it does is far greater than just that awkward silence afterward.

Recruiters who leave candidates in limbo, HR departments that never follow up after interviews, colleagues who leave emails unanswered indefinitely, and employees who vanish without notice contribute to the erosion of trust and professionalism in the workplace.

At its core, ghosting signals a lack of respect and emotional maturity. Whether it's a hiring manager refusing to update a candidate, a new hire who stops responding after signing an offer, or an executive who ignores follow-up emails, the result is the same: confusion, frustration, and resentment. The worst part is that it can be

---

[20] "Research from CommBank Reveals Why Gen Z Aren't Answering Your Call," *CommBank*, June 29, 2023.

contagious. Some people believe it's acceptable to do it because they've experienced ghosting from their employers.[21]

But in a professional setting, avoidance isn't an option, at least not if we want to build credibility and maintain strong working relationships. Clear, direct communication, even when it's uncomfortable, fosters trust and reliability. A simple acknowledgment such as "I haven't forgotten about this," or "I don't have an answer yet, but I'll update you soon," is better than silence and fosters respect.

We all know what it feels like to be left hanging. The uncertainty, overanalyzing, and second-guessing is frustrating and, frankly, unnecessary. If we expect others to value our time and contributions, we must extend the same courtesy. In business, besides being rude, ghosting can carry heavy emotional consequences,[22] and the "ghoster" may not realize they are damaging their brand by being perceived as cowardly.

Ultimately, more than lamenting the demise of the phone or the bad habits developed by asynchronous technology, the above observations show that there are large swaths of the population that have a very difficult time dealing with challenging interpersonal situations in real time, opting instead to shield themselves behind the anonymity of devices and platforms or just avoid them altogether. Being aware of these challenges can help leaders reflect on their own patterns as well as those of their teams.

---

[21] "Elon Professors Investigate the Rise of 'Ghosting' in Job Applications," *Elon University News*, November 14, 2024.

[22] Nuala Walsh, "Professional Ghosting: A Decision with Hidden Consequences," *Psychology Today*, April 2022.

Fostering a Culture of Connection

My brother managed a group of people at a large financial firm. He told me about an encounter he had with one of his team members. He approached "Pete" at the office, only to be met with irritation. Pete told him to please just send an interoffice chat message, and he'd get to the problem at the right time. My brother was surprised at this abrasiveness but calmly told Pete that the purpose of the hybrid office model was to be able to connect in person and take advantage of spontaneous team collaboration when they were there and they could leave the texting for when they were working remotely.

It seems that Pete found my brother's spontaneous approach intrusive, which may have been because he wasn't used to in-person business interactions. But once my brother explained his reasoning, Pete was encouraged to get out of his comfort zone.

I've heard several of my other clients note the gap in interpersonal skills revealed by several of their early career team members who recently entered the workforce. This generation wound up confined to a virtual environment during the COVID pandemic, right when they were supposed to be developing crucial soft skills such as communication, negotiating, networking, and conflict resolution. Many in this generation recognize some of their skills gap and admit to being reluctant to ask for help for fear of annoying their coworkers.[23] That's probably one of the reasons why Pete was put off by my brother's spontaneous approach.

---

[23] Hollie Castro, "How to Help Gen Z Employees Close the Gap on Soft Skills," *Quartz*, July 13, 2023.

A recent survey[24] highlighted how some employers prefer hiring older workers over recent college graduates. Many believe Gen Z struggles with workload management, punctuality, and deadlines. Some other behaviors include lack of eye contact, inappropriate dress and even bringing a parent to an interview.

Now, this isn't meant as a "What's wrong with young people nowadays?" rant. A senior HR professional I spoke to mentioned that Gen Z puts a lot of stock into emotions, likely due to the impact of social media and an over-reliance on devices that may have distorted their expectations of reality in the workplace.

Interpersonal intelligence, which includes skills such as empathy, effective communication, teamwork, and adaptability, is crucial for navigating today's workplace complexities. Pete's reaction to his manager might show why the idea of not bothering others is common among Gen Z. During the lockdowns, they learned to do most everything on their own, adopting a do-it-yourself approach. Asking for help might seem lazy or imposing for them. While this type of approach has helped forge an incredibly resourceful generation, sometimes asking someone directly can yield better results, along with fostering connection and trust.

One young career professional I met with mentioned that after having done things virtually for so long, he was cast out of his comfort zone when he was required to be on-site nine-to-five for an internship, where he was expected to dress professionally and communicate in a more formal manner in meetings and emails. He admitted that although suffering a bit of a culture shock at first, he

---

[24] Intelligent.com, "Nearly 4 in 10 Employers Avoid Hiring Recent College Grads in Favor of Older Workers," December 12, 2023.

managed to flow with the learning curve with a little patience and persistence.

His experience highlights a challenge many early-career professionals face as they transition into hybrid or in-person environments: bridging the gap between virtual habits and the interpersonal skills needed for workplace success. Managers play a crucial role in promoting confidence in interactions and fostering an environment where real-time collaboration thrives.

Leaders can help their team members gain confidence in their real-time communication by encouraging them to track how effective their interactions are over time. For instance, if they've exchanged multiple emails without making progress, suggest that they pivot to a phone or video call to resolve the issue more quickly.

They can also show appreciation when team members engage in spontaneous, real-time interactions and reinforce the value of interpersonal communication and collaboration. Sometimes the best solutions come from simple methods, such as making that call or stopping by someone's desk to hash things out.

Occasionally, all it takes is reassurance that those personal interactions are beneficial and desirable for optimal results. Managers can establish an easy-to-access culture by establishing an open-door policy. I always make it a point to let my clients, colleagues, and friends know they are always welcome to call without an appointment, that their calls are never an imposition or inconvenience, and if I can't answer immediately, I'll get back to them as soon as I can.

Recently, an acquaintance admitted she sometimes avoided client calls because she felt uncertain about having the answers on the spot. I reassured her that perfection isn't the expectation in spontaneous interactions. When people call out of the blue, they typically don't expect fully prepared responses.

Even if we say that we'll get back to the caller with an answer, we're still building rapport by showing that their call matters enough to interrupt our current activity. In our busy day to day, that willingness to engage, even briefly, is heartwarming. It reinforces that our interactions go beyond getting tasks done and speaks to our desire to strengthen relationships along the way.

Ultimately, integrating these practices ensures that teams are more connected and aligned with their goals, leading to increased productivity and satisfaction across the board.

Connection and Social Media

Here's an interesting exercise to try: The next time you're in a public area where you're waiting for something, look around. Chances are, everyone's head is down, their eyes glued to their device. It reminds me of a scene from the 2008 Disney Pixar movie WALL-E, in which everyone is riding on scooters and glued to their screens, oblivious to the fact that the person they are talking to is right next to them.

Which leads me to wonder: Has our comfort with digital interfaces grown so strong that it currently undermines our real-world connections? While technology has definitely enhanced how we communicate and work, there's an undeniable loss in spontaneity and authenticity when face-to-face interactions are replaced with screens.

Millennials and Gen Z grew up with social media, which let them connect with many more people, but this new tool has become a double-edged sword, leading to a false sense of connection and isolation. The influence of social media extends deeply into our emotional and mental well-being, shaping how we perceive ourselves and others. Understanding this impact is crucial because it forms the basis of how we build meaningful connections in an age dominated by virtual connections.

This brings me to the insights of social psychologist Jonathan Haidt, which I consider invaluable. In his book *The Anxious Generation*, Haidt's research sheds light on the impact of social media on adolescent mental health, particularly among Gen Z, who suffer the highest numbers of mental health issues.[25] According to Haidt, the excessive use of social media, combined with overprotective parenting, has contributed to increased rates of anxiety and depression among this generation.

He specifically points to the years between 2010 and 2015, when social media usage exploded. This was a turning point which he calls "the great rewiring" when young people began to isolate themselves rather than engage in real-life interactions.

While social media has done a wonderful job of connecting us with people and helping us market our brands and showcase our lives, the feelings of inadequacy that surge from comparing ourselves to others can be quite devastating. Tristan Harris, founder of the Center for Humane Technology and creator of the Netflix documentary "*The Social Dilemma*" points out that social media's

---

[25] American Psychological Association, *Stress in America: Generation Z* (Washington, DC: American Psychological Association, 2018).

aim to maximize engagement has led to unforeseen consequences, including addiction, depression[26] and polarization.

In her book, *Alone Together: Why We Need to Talk More than Ever,* Sherry Turkle explains how our overreliance on technology for communication is eroding our ability to engage in deep and meaningful conversations. The superficial nature of online interaction also erodes empathy, as we mindlessly scroll through feeds and consume information without being able to understand and relate to the experiences of others.

Whenever I talk to individuals about their experience with social media, I hear the same mixed feelings. There seems to be an apparent consensus that it is a necessary evil, but lately I've detected a shift toward awareness of the consequences of mindless consumption. The dopamine rush is hard to overcome. But just as we know that it's unhealthy to consume massive amounts of sugar or simple carbs, we must be mindful of our consumption of social media.

Adolescents are not the only ones suffering the consequences. Sometimes as I scroll through social media and look at other posts, I can't help but compare myself and feel a surge of impostor syndrome as I see others bragging about their accomplishments. Several colleagues have confessed the same—including my mentor, who is an extremely successful professional speaker. If you have social media, chances are you have felt this at some point too.

It's not a coincidence that many successful people recommend temperance in the use of social media. Though it can be difficult to

---

[26] McLean Hospital, "Is It or Isn't It? How Social Media Is Affecting Your Mental Health," October 4, 2022.

break old habits, I have found that when I want to reach for my phone to start scrolling, I remember some of the suggestions I've read or heard about, such as:

- **Taking digital detox breaks:** My daughter often finds the need to uninstall certain social media apps for a while when she starts feeling inadequate due to all her friends having a better time than her, (or so she thinks) and then she might re-install it over the weekend.
- **Setting tech-free zones:** The dinner table should be a tech-free zone. When we are being spoken to by a family member, friend, or colleague, it's time to put the phone down. I've had more than one family conflict because of someone looking at their phone at the dinner table.

When it comes to missed opportunities for connection, many fail to see the obvious. We will never get to our death bed and wish we had scrolled more and ignored our family more. Time flies. Our kids grow. Let's make sure we're there to witness it.

- **Feed curation:** Interestingly, I've found that during those down times from social media, I have had some ideas for new projects which have led me to do more research and consume more educational content, to wonderful results. I've discovered resources and been impressed with how generous people are with their knowledge. My research with AI led me to many fascinating discoveries, and I count myself privileged to live in this fascinating time.

When it comes down to it, social media can be a powerful tool for connection and information but must be used mindfully so it doesn't atrophy our communication skills. Even simple, incremental changes, such as those suggested by James Clear in his popular book *Atomic Habits* can make a great difference in our lives as they compound over time to create significant results.

Media consumption habits carry over into how people show up at work. We start to accept distraction and shallow engagement as the norm. The constant interruptions can cause attention fragmentation, which makes it increasingly difficult for people to focus for long periods, reflect deeply or integrate experiences. For a team to function, we need all of those, and a culture that fosters them.

The goal isn't to eliminate technology, of course, but to find a healthy balance. As leaders, we set the tone for how teams engage. When we use digital tools with intention and protect time for real conversation, we create space for deeper connection. Remember, connection requires intentional presence, not constant contact.

> Connection requires intentional presence, not constant contact.

Being present helps us reach a crucial goal: building rapport.

Building Rapport in a Digital Age

I was on a flight from Mexico City to Guadalajara when I noticed the woman sitting next to me reading a novel I recognized. I couldn't help myself and said, "Oh, that's a good book. Are you enjoying it?" She smiled and shared that she was, and we started a very pleasant conversation that lasted the rest of the flight. As it turned out, we were staying at the same hotel, so we shared a taxi ride from the airport, had dinner and continued our conversation.

We found out we shared a few things in common, such as kids the same age and similar philosophies toward life. We exchanged information and a few weeks later I got a call from the Learning and Development manager at her company who asked if I could come in to talk about some leadership skills programs. That company became a steady client of mine for years, and my travel acquaintance became a good friend. It all started with a comment about a book.

Connecting with people can be extremely satisfying and rewarding. It may be a brief connection like a smile, chuckle, or comment, or a longer conversation. The problem is that, by constantly looking at our devices and wearing earbuds (or headphones), we're literally shutting ourselves off from the real people around us in favor of virtual presences far away. How many opportunities do we miss out on every day?

More and more, casual conversations with strangers or even acquaintances are becoming a fading memory. Restaurants are filled with diners silently scrolling, teens sitting together, looking down at their phones instead of each other, and face-to-face interactions interrupted by constant checks of our electronic appendages. This decline in attentiveness has real consequences. Meaningful connections are built on shared experiences and genuine interest in others. These qualities are difficult to cultivate when our focus is constantly divided.

Those instant connections to people and the discovery that we have something in common with a stranger can be heartwarming, like with my airplane friend. It's something we desperately need in the current social and political climate, which seems to be separating us more and more, even as we gain the ability to connect to people further and further away. It's healthy and beneficial in so many ways and builds a sense of solidarity and community.

Don't Knock the Small Talk

Recently I found an article that stated that in a poll of two thousand employed adults, 74 percent struggle to make small talk with their co-workers. Many even avoid going into common areas just to avoid partaking in the practice. A young woman recently posted a video saying how small talk is so "cringe" but remains an unpleasant skill that must be developed the way one exercises one's muscles.

Interesting. I find it a little sad that people suffer through interactions and feel them to be so tedious. But ok, maybe it's not a favorite activity, but navigating and connecting to someone we don't know is an important skill to develop. Practice can help foster empathy and listening skills, not to mention create rapport for better influence and persuasion. And who knows, we may be pleasantly surprised at the end of the interaction. Did I mention that effective leaders do this particularly well? It's a skill that desperately requires mastership, especially with everyone burying their noses in their devices.

Furthermore, we know that AI has been a huge disruptor to our society, much in the same way that advancements in technology have been throughout humanity. From agriculture to industrialization, to knowledge. Currently, much of the knowledge economy is being replaced by the relationship or human economy[27] with the rise of AI.

Previously, value came from intellectual capital, with knowledge workers solving problems with their expertise. However, as AI increasingly manages these knowledge-based tasks efficiently, humans must shift their focus to the uniquely human aspects that AI can't replicate as easily, such as relationship building, emotional intelligence and complex interpersonal interactions.

This is a particularly important skill for leaders, as we need to help teams not only adapt to AI but also strengthen interpersonal dynamics to maintain competitiveness in this new landscape. The ability to foster relationships and apply human judgment and critical thinking is what sets people apart in today's economy.

The broader trend calls for blending AI proficiency with uniquely human capabilities. To practice this rapport building in our interactions every day, we can:

- **Start Small/Ask Open Ended Questions**

   We don't need to pressure ourselves to launch into deep philosophical discussions. We can begin with a simple hello, a smile, observation or question. People are happy to answer a question where they sense genuine interest. Find a reason to engage.

---

[27] Aneesh Raman, and Maria Flynn, "When Your Technical Skills Are Eclipsed, Your Humanity Will Matter More Than Ever," *New York Times*, February 14, 2024.

- **Focus on the Other Person**

  Shyness is often the result of self-consciousness. Once we start talking, we can shift our attention to the other person. We can ask them about themselves. Open-ended questions usually work best, as they let the other person share in a non-restrictive way and don't sound like interrogation.

- **Find Common Ground**

  We can look for shared experiences. If we're standing in a line waiting for something, we can bring the common experience to the forefront and move on from there. When I saw the woman reading a book I previously enjoyed, I felt the connection over something we had in common.

- **Project Confidence**

  An air of friendliness and openness is contagious. A warm greeting, paired with eye contact and a smile, can work wonders and create reciprocity.

- **Be Okay with Rejection**

  Sometimes people are just not interested in having a conversation. Oh well! Their loss.... Next!

With our world increasingly dominated by screens, the art of conversation is a critical skill that must actively be cultivated, much in the same way that practicing a foreign language is essential to keep our abilities to speak it fresh. You know the saying: If you don't use it, you lose it!

Hardwired for Connection

One day, while my son was a toddler and I was busy in the kitchen, I accidentally dropped a glass and watched it shatter. Frustrated, I let out an expletive. When he yelled the same exact word to me, I couldn't help bursting into laughter, while thinking that I wasn't providing a very good example for him. Funny how kids say the darndest things! If you've ever spent time around young children, I'm sure you've seen how they mimic those around them, usually family members, sometimes with tender results and sometimes in a way that casts a mirror on our shortcomings.

That natural inclination of babies to mimic their parents plays a crucial role in the early stages of social interaction. This imitation not only helps young children bond with their caregivers[28] but also starts the process of learning social cues and emotional responses.

These interactions are critical for the development of trust and security, aligning with the biological need for connection to ensure survival and emotional development. But these early interactions are also laden with oxytocin release, often referred to as the "love hormone," which reinforces the bonding process and decreases stress and anxiety in the child. This biological response to social interaction highlights the inherent need for human connection right from the beginning of life.

Our desire for connection isn't just a "nice to have;" it's woven into the very fabric of our being. On a biological level, human connection is essential for survival. Evolution has shaped us as social

---

[28] Ruth Feldman, Ilanit Gordon, Moran Influs, Tamar Gutbir, and Richard P. Ebstein. "Parental Oxytocin and Early Caregiving Jointly Shape Children's Oxytocin Response and Social Reciprocity," *Neuropsychopharmacology* 38 no. 4 (2013): 1154–62.

creatures, reliant on each other for safety, food acquisition, and raising offspring[29]. This phenomenon has been studied from anthropological, psychological, neuroscientific, sociological, and economic perspectives.

When we interact meaningfully with others, our brains release a cascade of feel-good chemicals. Oxytocin, mentioned before, is a key player. It fosters feelings of trust and bonding and reduces stress and anxiety. Dopamine, associated with reward and motivation, also releases during positive social interactions, encouraging us to seek out more connection.

As children grow, they begin to extend their trust and social skills beyond their primary caregivers to include peers and teachers. The skills learned through early connection, such as empathy, trust, and communication, are further developed through play and educational activities. Social connections in childhood are crucial for developing self-esteem and a sense of belonging.

As we enter adolescence, social needs and connections become more complex and take on new forms. The typical teenage angst depicted in countless movies about acceptance and belonging throughout generations illustrates this transitional life phase. We can see it in *Grease* in the '70's with Sandy adopting a new persona to entice Danny to date her, in *The Breakfast Club* in the '80's, as the kids get past biases about each other, or the cliques shown in *Mean Girls* in the aughts. It's always the same theme, driven by an evolutionary need to fit into a group—a trait that once ensured survival.

---

[29] Annie Swanepoel, et al, "How Evolution Can Help Us Understand Child Development and Behaviour," *BJPsych Advances* 24, no. 5 (2018): 306-315.

We humans are social creatures. Relationships help us thrive, be healthier and live longer.[30] Studies tell us that relationships provide support in two primary ways: as a source of strength during adversity and as a means for thriving at other times. Given these insights, the relevance of fostering strong interpersonal relationships in the workplace becomes more important. In professional settings, where stress and challenges are commonplace, robust social connections can help us feel more capable of managing stress, not to mention enhance our overall job satisfaction and productivity.

Interestingly, Gallup conducted a study[31] that showed that having a "best friend" at work not only enriches the work experience but also contributes significantly to an employee's performance and well-being. Employees with close friendships at work are more likely to be deeply involved in their jobs, putting in extra effort and demonstrating higher performance levels. These friendships offer professional support as well as personal encouragement and understanding, which can be so helpful in times of stress or challenging projects. They can promote creative problem-solving, too.

Leaders can foster a workplace where friendships flourish and team members feel valued by intentionally promoting connection and support. Think of the acronym L.E.A.D.— Linking People, Establishing Alignment, Acknowledging Achievements and Driving Engagement —to create strategies that nurture team relationships and build a thriving work environment.

---

[30] "Could Social Relationships be Key to Reaching Healthy Longevity?" *National Library of Medicine*, 15, no. 12 (2023).

[31] Alok Patel and Stephani Plowman, "The Increasing Importance of a Best Friend at Work", *Gallup*, January 19, 2024.

L.E.A.D. for Connection

L—Linking People: Foster a Sense of Connection and Solidarity

Fostering connections among team members is essential to a supportive work environment. These connections can be strengthened through activities ranging from casual social gatherings—think lunches, birthday acknowledgements, or outings—to structured workshops focused on collaboration or problem-solving. Whether casual or structured, team building activities play a crucial role in building trust and camaraderie beyond just work tasks.

Some leaders opt for organized structured teambuilding workshops to strengthen team bonds. The programs can include built-in skill-building activities in the guise of fun challenges to foster collaboration, problem-solving, or trust. When I conduct these types of sessions, I find it's great to see adults laugh and let their inner child emerge as they tackle creative, sometimes whimsical challenges.

For example, one activity I conduct requires participants to stand in a circle, each holding a tennis ball. Their task is to pass the ball to the person on their right while simultaneously receiving another ball from their left. At first, chaos ensues, but with time, the group learns to coordinate and create a "perfect gear." This fun exercise highlights the importance of communication, strategy, consensus, and leadership.

Another activity involves five people tasked with tying three knots with a long rope. Each member can use only one hand to hold the rope, with strict instructions to not let go. Participants must brainstorm and work different iterations until they achieve their goal within the allotted time.

The activities are usually simple, but afterward, the magic happens, as participants share insights into workplace dynamics. It's enlightening to see the analogies made when comparing the activity to real-life scenarios. Some may reflect on the errors that reminded them of a recent lack of communication flow at work, or of acting too soon without obtaining buy-in from stakeholders.

Many powerful reflections emerge and help break down barriers, especially those formed during periods of stress. Such reflections foster genuine empathy and camaraderie. The lightbulbs seem to go off as participants consider similar situations in their day-to-day and remember how they overcame some of those challenges in the game. Some resources for ideas for teambuilding activities can be found in the book *"Quick Team-Building Activities for Busy Managers"* by Brian Cole Miller or in *"The Big Book of Team-Building Games"* by John W. Newstrom.

When working remotely, leaders can still conduct several exercises to get their team members to break the ice and get to know each other. In my sessions, I often use such icebreaker activities such as asking participants to post a picture of a favorite activity on our virtual board or posing fun questions like, "If you were a cartoon character, who would you be and why?" Appendix D provides a list of questions you can sample for your team. These small actions spark conversations and build personal connections.

Whether in-person or virtual, the goal of team-building activities is to deepen connections not just professionally but personally as well. When participants laugh together, share stories, or tackle challenges as a group, they build a foundation of trust and belonging. This, in turn, enhances communication, collaboration, and frankly, overall job satisfaction. By prioritizing these activities, leaders create an environment where individuals feel valued and motivated to contribute their best.

E — Establish Alignment: Implement Regular Check-Ins and Feedback Sessions

Building alignment within a team starts with open, consistent communication. Regular one-on-one check-ins provide a valuable opportunity for leaders to connect with their team members on both a personal and professional level.

Sadly, I have seen organizations in which one-on-ones only happen during performance evaluations, which can seem impersonal and reactive. I often remind leaders that scheduling frequent, informal check-ins helps foster trust, provide ongoing support and create opportunities to celebrate small wins.

Regular check-ins also allow managers to adopt a situational leadership style[32]. For example, a new hire may need more guidance and hands-on support, while a seasoned team member might benefit from autonomy and high-level strategic discussions. By tailoring these interactions to the individual's needs, leaders can ensure that their team members feel supported and valued at every stage of their journey. Of course, the only certain way to find the right approach involves exploring the knowledge and motivation (skill and will) of each team member.

---

[32] Paul Hersey and Kenneth H. Blanchard. *Management of Organizational Behavior: Utilizing Human Resources.* 3rd ed. (Englewood Cliffs, NJ: Prentice-Hall, 1977).

Frequent check-ins also foster a culture of feedback. Managers can harness these sessions to provide constructive feedback in a timely manner, ensuring issues are addressed before they escalate. Equally important is recognizing progress.

While helpful to have a loose agenda for check-ins, i.e. walking into the meeting with a checklist covering priorities, challenges, and upcoming tasks, it's just as important to allow space for unstructured conversations. These moments can uncover hidden concerns or aspirations that might not emerge in a formal setting. A simple question such as, "What's been on your mind lately?" can lead to deeper insights into what a team member is feeling or might need to thrive.

Beyond one-on-one meetings, holding regular team check-ins can ensure everyone stays on the same page. These sessions can include progress updates, collaborative goal setting, or even a quick round of sharing wins and challenges. For remote teams, tools such as shared dashboards or virtual whiteboards can make these meetings more interactive and engaging.

Practical Tips for Successful Check-Ins:

- Schedule meetings at consistent intervals to create predictability and routine.
- Use active listening techniques like paraphrasing to show genuine interest and understanding.
- Balance discussions between current challenges and long-term goals.
- Close each check-in with actionable steps or next steps to provide clarity and momentum.

By making alignment a regular practice, managers can strengthen relationships with their team members and foster a culture of clarity and accountability. This intentional focus on alignment helps create a sense of shared purpose and ensures that every team member feels their contributions matter.

Acknowledging Achievements: Create a Culture of Recognition

We've talked about how recognition plays a crucial role in motivating people within teams and reinforcing positive behaviors. A great way to recognize team members is through reflective recognition.[33] This approach involves creating opportunities for employees to reflect on and share their accomplishments, challenges, and growth.

For example, leaders can encourage team members to share what they've been working on and what they're most proud of during team meetings or one-on-one check-ins. Team members can also be encouraged to discuss the hardest part of their job and how they've navigated it. This highlights resilience while promoting empathy and support from colleagues.

Recognition has a ripple effect on the entire team. When leaders model consistent recognition, it encourages team members to follow suit, creating a culture where appreciation becomes a shared responsibility. Over time, this culture can transform the workplace into a space where team members feel empowered and inspired to contribute their best.

---

[33] Christopher Littlefield. "A Better Way to Recognize Your Employees." *Harvard Business Review*, October 25, 2022.

D—Driving Engagement: Promote Open Communication and Collaboration

Engagement is the cornerstone of a thriving workplace. With more teams working remotely, it's crucial to find ways to foster engagement through creative strategies. In remote or hybrid teams, we can incorporate activities to add a human touch to virtual interaction, such as sharing personal highlights on an interactive platform.

Open communication helps foster engagement. Team members who feel valued and heard become more likely to participate actively and give it their all. Regular brainstorming sessions create a perfect arena for team members to voice ideas, concerns, or suggestions. This ensures commitment once decisions are made over the next steps.

Team collaboration across functional areas also improves results within an organization. A young marketing coordinator told me that she would regularly schedule meetings with the sales team to brainstorm and exchange ideas before deciding on specific courses of action, which not only ensured alignment for smoother execution, but also taught her a lot about the industry.

By implementing L.E.A.D: Linking People, Establishing Alignment, Acknowledging Achievements, and Driving Engagement, leaders can effectively foster relationships within their teams. This approach helps enhance workplace dynamics and contributes to a more productive and fulfilling work experience for everyone involved.

Summary: The Knots that Block Connection

The rules of engagement have changed in the digital age and limited our ability to create rapport. As we've seen, the ease of texting and digital messaging has led to a decline in the spontaneous, real-time conversations that help foster genuine connections. Reluctance in engaging in phone calls or face-to-face discussions, particularly among younger generations, has created a ripple effect on both personal and professional settings, leading to a loss of essential interpersonal skills.

This isn't about not using our phones as phones anymore or avoiding contact with strangers. It's also about missing opportunities to build rapport, establish trust, and engage meaningfully with others. Whether we realize it or not, these avoidances eliminate opportunities for professional collaboration or moments of shared humanity, which carry a real cost.

Untangling the Knots:

The key takeaway is that while digital communication has its benefits, it's crucial to reintroduce and prioritize real-time, human connections—both in our personal lives and in the workplace. This means being mindful of our chosen means of communication, being accountable and respectful in our responses and creating rapport with our colleagues in an effort to promote trust and collaboration.

By practicing the L.E.A.D. model, leaders can help their teams rediscover the value of human connection, driving better communication, deeper relationships, and a more cohesive work environment. Ultimately, the aim is to strike a balance between the convenience of digital tools and the irreplaceable value of face-to-face interactions.

That's why it helps to have a clear, repeatable process, so we can pause, reflect and respond with purpose instead of on autopilot.

We'll be exploring the CLEAR model, a simple but powerful framework that helps us slow down, get grounded and communicate in a way that builds trust and clarity, even when things feel messy.

Communication works for those who work at it.

— John Powell

CHAPTER 6

Untangling Communication

The Underlying Message

My son, Marco, suddenly started having seizures when he was three and was diagnosed with idiopathic epilepsy. As time passed, the seizures started affecting his cognitive abilities, and I suspect the medications contributed to the behavioral issues that followed. It was a trying time, and I found myself often struggling to communicate with him, growing frustrated and impatient.

But as I looked back, I realized that most times I was talking *at* him, not *to* him. I was trying to get things done, to get him to take his medication, to behave, to sit still, to do or not do this or that. My interactions were transactional, driven by my need to manage his behavior and stay in control. I struggled tremendously when he wouldn't listen to me, convinced that he wasn't understanding. The thing is, he did understand me, more than I gave him credit for. I was just underestimating the depth of his comprehension. To say it was difficult would have been an understatement, and it took quite a bit of self-reflection and self-awareness to finally change my mindset and approach.

At one period, while he was ten, we tried the ketogenic diet in the hopes of reducing his seizures. It was a brutal diet, with large amounts of fat and protein, all of which had to be measured and weighed to keep him in a state of ketosis, with almost zero carbohydrates. One day, we had all gone out to eat. I brought

Marco's meal with me, but his sister was eating something different, and he wanted some.

I braced myself for the storm as he reached for her French fries, but I decided to look him in the eye and try to connect at a different level. I stopped giving instructions and just started talking about how difficult it was to deal with seizures, how I knew what a great sacrifice he was making, and his level of discipline, and how much I admired that. I was surprised that he paused and actually listened to me. It wasn't a miracle breakthrough, but it was a start.

I'm probably not the only person to experience the challenge of connecting with someone, of feeling as if that other person and I are living in two different, impenetrable bubbles and struggling to communicate. To complicate things further, when we are under stress or pressure, we tend to double down on the issue and forget about the person. Could it be that we get caught up in the transactional nature of our message and overlook the importance of the emotional element?

That thought makes me recall the great-grand father of books on interpersonal intelligence, the classic "How to Win Friends and Influence People," first published in 1936. I remember clearly how Dale Carnegie stressed the importance of making the other person feel important and doing so sincerely. It's a principle echoed by Mary Kay Ash, the successful founder of Mary Kay Cosmetics, who once said that we should imagine every person with an invisible sign around their neck that says, "Make me feel important". It's such a simple piece of advice that when practiced sincerely, can make a world of difference.

Despite how much I love my son, the way I was communicating probably didn't reflect that. My message was no doubt more like, "Please don't make my life more difficult," which is something we unintentionally transmit many times in our day-to-day interactions. We are usually more concerned with what we can get out of the interaction than the needs of the other person. But we can change that and thus, change the outcome.

My experience with my special needs son was a great motivator; I knew I needed a way to connect more effectively with him. At the same time, I would hear my clients express exasperation with their communication struggles, which included misaligned expectations and difficulty transmitting urgency, setting boundaries, and reaching agreements.

If we think about it, most of the "knots" in our interactions aren't caused by a lack of technical skills. They stem from misaligned expectations or lack of clarity. No matter how skilled someone is at problem-solving, people are not problems to be solved. We all have our unique perspectives, emotional baggage, triggers and filters. Understanding each other is the key to moving forward in our relationships or tasks, or both.

> No matter how skilled someone is at problem-solving, people are not problems to be solved.

Sometimes we get stuck in problem-solving mode, trying to manage our way through challenges while ignoring the human element of the knot, spinning our wheels in an endless cycle. Yet sometimes the best way to untangle a knot is to pause and stop tugging at it. To take a breath and remember that behind every problem is a person with fears, frustrations, and needs just like us.

So, let's take that step back and look at the knot with a clear head. If we want to untangle it, we must understand how the threads got twisted in the first place. By gently following one end of the string, we can trace where it leads and slowly begin to loosen what's stuck.

The Communication Process

If you've ever taken a communication class, you've probably heard this basic breakdown of the process: There's a sender, a message, and a receiver. On paper it sounds simple, but in real life, nothing about communication is that linear or clean. The moment two people enter the equation, things get complicated. Each person brings their perspective, experience, culture, personality and assumptions into every interaction.

Just like a knot, what seems like a single strand of miscommunication is often a tangle of missed cues, mixed messages and expectations. Understanding the process is the first step toward understanding and clarity.

As you can see in the diagram below, all these elements shape how we think and process (encode) our message. Then we must transmit it to someone who in turn must interpret (decode) the message through their lens, perspective, experience, culture, personality and assumptions.

Along the way, any number of factors can create "noise"—things that distort or obscure the original intent. It's a delicate process, and the original message may or may not reach its destination intact. Anyone who has ever played the childhood game "Whisper down the lane" has seen how quickly the message can get garbled, even in the simplest of scenarios.

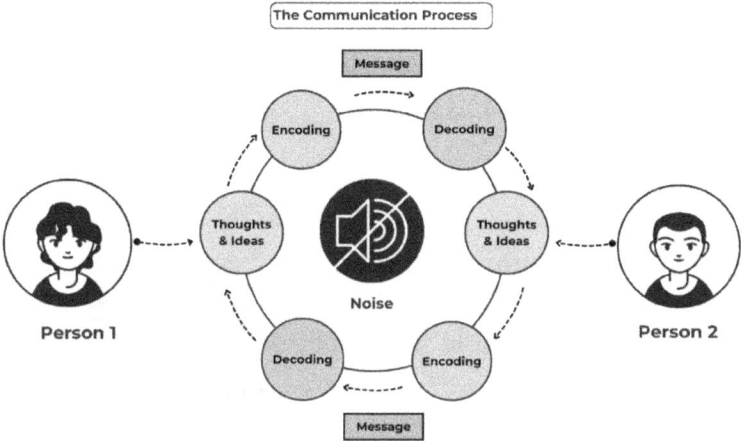

The thing is that communication is more than a classroom concept or child's game. It's real life, and it plays out every day in meetings, emails, project updates and casual chats. Miscommunication is rarely the consequence of lack of intent; it usually occurs when what one person meant to say wasn't exactly what the other person heard.

One of the biggest challenges many leaders and their teams face is transmitting what's in their head, hoping it sounds as they intended and lands just right. Unfortunately, things don't always come out perfectly tailored to the receiver. Developing a structure can help decrease misunderstandings.

To bridge that gap and help my clients craft more intentional messages and be more effective in their everyday communication, I have developed a simple, practical framework I call CLEAR. This model works as a general template or "best practice" in both personal and professional settings.

It's not a script or rigid formula, but simply a guide to prevent tangles in communication and refocus on the core elements that actually move the needle. Each letter stands for the principle that can be used to make sure our message is both sent and received in a way that fosters clarity, trust, and action.

Let's walk through it.

Everyday CLEAR Communication

Whether speaking to people in our personal or professional circle, we can take steps to ensure our conversations flow naturally and successfully.

First, we must:

Convey Context

This step has really made my life easier. Beginning a conversation by sharing what we're thinking or why we want to do something makes it much more likely that the other person will align with us rather than resist us.

Sharing our "why," as leadership expert Simon Sinek famously put it, is a form of respect. By explaining our reasoning, we extend courtesy to our receiver. In this way, we reveal before requesting, which prevents guesswork and confusion. There's a touch of vulnerability involved, which communicates, "Here's what I'm hoping for," and that softens the space between people by making the interaction more authentic.

This principle has made communication with my son Marco so much easier and deeper. When he reached for his sister's food, instead of assuming that he wouldn't understand or care about my intent, I told him my "why." I was worried about his health, was hoping the ketogenic diet would work like medicine to reduce his seizures, and I didn't want him to have a seizure and hurt himself again. Just like that, he withdrew his hand. He understood and aligned. No drama, all because I took the time to share my context instead of simply issuing a "No".

The same approach works in the workplace, though we often forget to apply it. Take for instance, a manager who asks a team member to redo a report. Without context, the request may come across as arbitrary, controlling or even dismissive of the effort already made. But a slight shift changes everything:

We're presenting to the regional VP next week and I want to make sure we highlight the results that speak most to her priorities. She's very data-focused, so it would be great for you to revisit the report and make some tweaks so we can make a stronger impact.

Now, instead of feeling micromanaged, the team member understands the why and the context behind our request. They see the bigger picture and are more likely to feel like a partner working toward a shared outcome rather than someone being corrected or second-guessed.

Sharing context may seem to lengthen the communication process, but not really. If we skip this step and get resistance or pushback, we'll often end up having to explain why later, and by then, the conversation may already be off track. So instead of reacting, we're just changing the order of things and offering a couple of thoughtful sentences upfront that will probably save us time, energy and misunderstanding in the long run.

It's not necessary to give a lecture or narrate our inner monologue. Just a couple of intentional sentences is all it takes to frame our message with purpose and direction. When we reveal before we request, we build clarity. When we share the bigger picture, we foster solidarity. That's the first step in untangling communication.

Listen Actively

If there's one skill that seems deceptively simple but is rarely mastered, it's listening. We've probably heard all the cliches about listening, like how we have two ears and only one mouth for a reason, and yet truly good listeners are hard to come by. A good leader learns how to listen to identify patterns, pivot, strategize, negotiate, and coach.

When I work with leaders on coaching skills, for example, this is the part that trips them up the most. They're eager to help, and their instinct is to offer advice, share their opinion, or suggest a solution. It comes from a good place, but it often short-circuits the process, because in rushing to respond, they miss what's really being said.

The heart of coaching isn't about having the answers (even if we're sure we do), but rather about developing the person in front of us. The purpose is to foster reflection, support growth, and guide team members as they arrive at their own solutions. If we do the thinking for them, the learning doesn't happen, and we've lost the opportunity to develop them, making it easier for the team member to continue to "delegate upward."

Great coaching is hard. It requires prudence, patience, and lots of listening. It's the practice of helping others become the protagonist of their own story instead of trying to be the hero of every conversation.

That's why listening isn't passive; it requires active, deliberate work. The goal is to go beyond hearing the words and uncover meaning which can live underneath the surface and be buried under frustration, hesitation or self-doubt.

For example, when someone vents about a difficult colleague or an overwhelming workload, the real message may not be about the other person or the pile of tasks. It may be about feeling unsupported or unsure. If we jump too fast with solutions, we may end up solving the wrong problem or even making them feel unheard.

Even in high-stakes environments, listening is a strategic advantage. Harvard's Program on Negotiation found that top negotiators spent significantly more time listening than their average counterparts[34]. Know why? Because you can't propose a better solution if you don't fully understand what the other side values or needs. Negotiating positions at a superficial level rarely gets you far.

In coaching, it's the same thing. When we listen actively, by paraphrasing what we've heard, asking open-ended questions, and resisting the urge to hijack the conversation, we create space for others to think so that they can grow.

Empathize

Empathy has become one of those buzzwords that gets thrown around so often, it's easy to forget what it really looks like. We talked about it earlier when we reviewed emotional intelligence, but it's worth revisiting here, because empathy goes beyond being a fluffy ideal. It's a mindset shift that can change the entire course of a conversation.

---

[34] Harvard Law School Program on Negotiation, "Negotiation Skills for Win-Win Negotiations," *The Program on Negotiation Daily Blog*, July 10, 2023.

Listening and empathy go hand in hand. When we're truly listening by paraphrasing what someone says, asking open-ended questions, or resisting the urge to fix or respond, we're already making space for empathy to grow. We can't help but try to understand the other person when we do those things. Empathy takes place when we've stayed present long enough to actually feel what the other person might be going through.

I know many might think that empathy includes outward dramatic displays of concern or polished statements such as, "I understand how you feel." But it's way more subtle and far more internal. Empathy involves shifting our lens and being willing to change our narrative.

Here's a simple example.

Let's say a colleague misses a deadline and seems defensive when you bring it up. The instinct might be to press them harder or point out the impact their delay had on the team. But what if we asked a different kind of question?

I noticed you seemed overwhelmed this week. Is there something going on that's made things harder?

That one question, rooted in curiosity, not blame, can open the door to understanding. Maybe they're dealing with a personal issue, or didn't have the resources they needed. We're not excusing the missed deadline; we're just showing that we care enough to understand the full picture before jumping in with feedback or next steps. This creates a spirit of collaboration and alliance instead of defensiveness and opposition.

Empathy is what prepares us, mentally and emotionally, for what comes next. It grounds us and reminds us that communication is about authentic connection. It can't be performative, because when it's fake, people sense it instantly.

Naturally, empathy helps us see things from the other person's perspective, but insight on its own doesn't always create an impact. Once we begin to understand where someone is coming from, the next step is figuring out how to respond in a way that fits the moment by going beyond what we feel and using our awareness to shape our approach so that the message lands with clarity and care.

Adjust

If empathy is the inner shift that helps us connect, adjusting is the outer shift that helps us land our message.

Once we've listened carefully and made the effort to understand someone's point of view, we're on the road responding with intention. Adjusting means using everything we've picked up through observation, like tone, mood, personality, culture and unspoken cues, to shape how we communicate moving forward.

Many professionals spend years trying to master this step. It's the reason so many assessments exist, from classics such as DISC and Myers Briggs to cultural intelligence tools and behavioral models. Deep down, we all want to be effective. We want our message to be heard and understood, and we want to minimize the friction that gets in the way.

Adjusting communication is a bit like translating from one language to another. Sometimes it's literal; for example, when I hear someone struggling in English and recognize they're Hispanic, I switch to Spanish to facilitate our exchange. But often it's more subtle. It's about making the message easier for the other person to process, in a way that feels natural and accessible to them. The meaning stays the same, but the delivery changes to match their style, pace or preference so that it doesn't get lost in translation.

For example, if you're naturally energetic and expressive, it may be second nature for you to jump right into ideas in meetings, brainstorm out loud and think on your feet. That may work well, but if there's someone on your team more deliberate or analytical, they may not feel comfortable "thinking out loud." An alternative approach could be:

I'd love your input on this idea, but feel free to take a little time and send me your thoughts later if that's easier.

I've seen this play out in my own interactions. My natural style is friendly, direct and high energy. But when I communicate with someone more reserved and thoughtful, I know I need to slow down, get to the point, and give them space to process so that my message is not just heard but actually received.

We all have default styles, and in many cases, they serve us well. But communication isn't one-size-fits-all. When we adjust our approach to suit the person or situation, we're not being inauthentic, but thoughtful, and that will often determine whether collaboration moves forward or breaks down.

Once we've adjusted how we communicate to better suit the person in front of us, we have one final opportunity to shape the conversation, and that's in how we frame our message. The way we present an idea, a correction, or even a disagreement can either close someone off or open them up.

Reframe Positively

Once we've given context, listened, empathized and adjusted our approach, the final step is shaping the message in a way that helps things move forward. Reframing positively is the moment when you show goodwill and a willingness to collaborate and move forward with solutions, focusing on what can be done rather than what can't.

When we're trying to solve a problem, give feedback, or move through a conflict, it's easy to get stuck in the past by rehashing what went wrong, who dropped the ball, or what should have happened. But that kind of backward-looking focus won't lead anywhere useful. In most cases, it just fuels defensiveness or discouragement.

A more productive approach is to ask, "Where do we go from here?" That simple shift helps the other person save face and keeps the conversation focused on a positive outcome. We're not ignoring the issue; we're redirecting energy toward something that can actually be built.

Rather than abandoning someone to their problem or shutting down the conversation, we can show solidarity. Further, we can balance our needs with that of the relationship by offering an alternative, suggesting a next step, or even just showing that we care about the outcome. Making that small shift away from finality and toward possibility can help promote collaboration.

For example, let's say a colleague asks for last-minute support on a report, but we're already stretched thin and can't take it on. A flat "Sorry, I can't help with that" ends the exchange. But reframing might sound like this:

I have a deadline I need to meet by the end of work today, but if you send me your draft, I can give it a quick read tomorrow morning and flag anything major. Or if it's super urgent, do you think George could help you?

The message is still a no to the original request, but it's a no with thought and goodwill. It acknowledges our limit while still offering something constructive.

The same applies in negotiation. When we listen carefully, we can probably pick up something the other person values that we may not have known at the start. That insight gives us a chance to reframe our proposal in a way that highlights shared interests or adds value based on what matters to them. Instead of, "Here's what I need," we can say:

Based on what you said about needing more visibility for your team, I think we could position this as a joint initiative. That way, your group gets the recognition it deserves, and we still hit the deadline on our side.

As you can see, reframing doesn't require us to bend over backward or try to please everyone. It's more about using everything we've learned in conversation—what they care about or are worried about and where there's flexibility—to craft a message that opens doors instead of closing them.

Download the CLEAR Communication Assessment and Cheat Sheet to help you apply the model to real conversations.

https://www.mariagaraitonandia.com/#clear

CONCLUSION
The Thread that Ties It All Together

Communication isn't always easy, but it's always worth the effort. When we take the time to share our context, listen with curiosity, empathize with sincerity, adjust with awareness, and reframe with purpose, we create the conditions for real connection. When people feel seen, heard, and understood, things start to move—projects, relationships, and even hearts. That's the power of untangling communication!

Back at the beginning, I asked you a few questions about your challenges:

- Is conflict ignored or escalated, making it harder for stakeholders to align and move forward?
- Do projects stall because of unclear communication or lack of meaningful feedback?
- Are there cross-cultural issues in your global teams that cause friction or misunderstandings?
- Are there sometimes generational disconnects that cause confusion or frustration among team members?
- Despite all the tools designed to connect us, are meaningful interactions with stakeholders still difficult to establish?

I didn't ask those questions rhetorically. I asked because I've seen the cost of ignoring them and I've seen the power of what happens when we take them seriously. Hopefully, you are now armed with the confidence and tools to face those challenges.

Throughout this book, we've explored the human side of communication, the part that lives between words, in tone, intent, and presence. We've looked at tools such as GAS, LEAD, CARE, FRAME, and CLEAR not as formulas, but as frameworks to help you make intentional choices. We've also acknowledged the knots—conflict, emotional triggers, cultural gaps, generational differences, use of technology—not as problems to avoid, but as invitations to listen more closely and lead more wisely.

You don't have to be perfect to be a great communicator. They say practice makes progress. You just need to be present and willing to engage to move forward.

Whether you're coaching your team through a tough season, navigating a merger, onboarding new colleagues, leading a remote team, or trying to figure out why people have stopped turning on their cameras, you now have a way to start: a path rooted in awareness and intention, with tools to foster dialogue and build trust.

I sometimes think back to my dad, struggling to connect in a culture that didn't match his style, feeling lost and alone despite his good intentions. I wish I could go back and hand him these tools, sit with him over coffee, and help him untangle what felt so frustrating at the time. I can't do that.

But I can share them with you.

So maybe someone else's father, or colleague, or team member, won't have to feel so lost. Learning how to untangle communication has changed my life in more ways than I can count. I hope it makes a difference in yours too.

Keep observing. Keep practicing. Keep untangling.

Let's Keep Untangling

If something in this book resonated with you, here are a few ways we can stay connected:

Grab Your Free Tools
Download the **Untangling Conflict Cheat Sheet** to keep the learning going.

Scan the QR code or visit:
www.globalbridgestraining.com/download-untangling-conflict-cheat-sheet

Take the **CLEAR Communication Assessment** and download the cheat sheet to reflect on your own communication style.

Scan the QR code or visit:

www.mariagaraitonandia.com/#clear

Bring This to Your Team

Want a keynote, workshop, or session for your team?
Let's make communication flow again.

www.mariagaraitonandia.com
Or connect on LinkedIn:
www.linkedin.com/in/mariagaraitonandia

Help Others Discover This Book

If this helped you, would you consider leaving a review?
A few words on Amazon can help someone else decide if it's right for them.

Or share it with a colleague or friend who could use a communication boost.

APPENDIX A

Is Your Team Tied Up in Knots? A Self-Diagnosis Tool

Evaluate how well your team communicates and collaborates by answering the following questions.

Choose the answer that best describes your usual team experience.

1. When different areas of your company need to collaborate, how well do they work together?

☐ A. Very well—they collaborate seamlessly.

☐ B. Sometimes—there are occasional challenges.

☐ C. Rarely—there's often tension or finger-pointing.

☐ D. They don't collaborate well—there's a lot of blame and pressure.

2. How frequently do conflicts arise within your team or between teams?

☐ A. Rarely—we manage conflicts as they come up.

☐ B. Sometimes—they're usually resolved quickly.

☐ C. Often—managers must get involved to resolve them.

☐ D. All the time—conflicts escalate and disrupt teamwork.

3. How comfortable are your team members with saying no or offering alternative solutions when they disagree?

☐ A. Very comfortable—they're assertive and proactive.

☐ B. Somewhat comfortable—though they tend to hesitate.

☐ C. Not very comfortable—they often say yes to avoid conflict.

☐ D. They almost never say no, even when it's necessary.

4. Do people in your team ignore or avoid addressing others' concerns or requests?

☐ A. Never—everyone communicates openly and respectfully.

☐ B. Occasionally—it's not a major issue.

☐ C. Often—people tend to ignore messages or requests.

☐ D. All the time—there's a clear disconnect between team members.

5. How does your team manage resolving conflicts without escalating them to management?

☐ A. Conflicts are resolved quickly at the team level.

☐ B. We manage them internally, though some escalate to managers.

☐ C. Conflicts often escalate, and managers must intervene.

☐ D. Most conflicts go straight to management for resolution.

6. Do team members work in silos or are they open to cross-functional collaboration?

☐ A. We collaborate across functions with no issues.

☐ B. Occasionally there are silos, but we manage to work around them.

☐ C. There's a noticeable silo mentality that hinders collaboration.

☐ D. We're entirely siloed, and it's a big obstacle to teamwork.

7. How confident is your team in offering constructive feedback when there's a problem?

☐ A. Very confident—feedback is given regularly and constructively.

☐ B. Somewhat confident, but feedback is often avoided.

☐ C. Not confident—feedback causes tension or is poorly received.

☐ D. We don't give feedback; issues are avoided or ignored.

8. How frequently do team members feel pressured by other areas instead of receiving support to solve problems together?

☐ A. Rarely—we support each other well.

☐ B. Occasionally—there's some pressure but nothing major.

☐ C. Often—teams blame or pressure each other instead of working together.

☐ D. It's a constant issue—teams are always shifting blame.

Scoring Guide

Count your answers and see which letter you choose most often.

Mostly A's: Your team has excellent communication and collaboration skills. Keep reinforcing these strengths.

Mostly B's: Your team does well in some areas but could improve in others. Consider targeted training or workshops.

Mostly C's: There are significant challenges in your team's communication. It's essential to address these issues to prevent further escalation.

Mostly D's: Your team struggles with severe communication issues. Comprehensive intervention, such as a restructuring of communication protocols or extensive training, may be necessary.

APPENDIX B

New Team Alignment Blueprint: Setting the Stage for Success

1. What's one unique thing about your culture that you'd like to share?
2. How do you prefer to receive feedback (e.g., written, verbal, direct, indirect)?
3. What's the best way to communicate with you when something is urgent?
4. How do you typically like to start your workday (e.g., quiet time, team check-in, coffee chat)?
5. When facing a challenge, what's your go-to problem-solving approach?
6. What's your favorite way to celebrate team successes?
7. How do you prefer to give and receive recognition?
8. What time zone do you work in, and how flexible is your schedule?
9. How do you feel about using video in meetings?
10. What's one thing you need from the team to be at your best?
11. If we are stuck on something, what's the best way for us to collaborate on a solution?

12. How do you balance work and personal time, especially when working remotely?

13. What's one thing that always helps you feel more connected to the team?

14. How do you prefer to handle misunderstandings or conflicts when they arise?

15. What's one cultural custom or tradition you'd like to share with the team?

16. How do you stay organized and manage your workload?

17. What's the best way for us to learn from each other's strengths?

18. What's a hobby or interest outside of work that you're passionate about?

19. How do you approach learning something new?

20. What can we do as a team to build and maintain trust, even across distances?

APPENDIX C

Cultural Snapshots: High-Context vs. Low-Context Communication

---

This self-assessment is designed to help you identify whether your communication style tends to align more with high-context or low-context cultures.

Answer each question based on how you typically interact with others in work and personal situations. At the end, you'll gain insight into your style and how it may affect your cross-cultural interactions.

You're working on a project with a team from several countries. During a virtual meeting, one member begins by greeting everyone individually and asking about their weekend before discussing the task. How do you respond?

☐ A) I think it's nice, but I prefer to get to the point more quickly.

☐ B) I engage in the conversation and see it as an important part of team building.

☐ C) I participate briefly but try to steer the conversation toward the task.

☐ D) I find it unnecessary and wait until the project discussion begins.

A colleague made a mistake that affected the project. How do you approach discussing it?

☐ A) I address the mistake directly and offer suggestions for avoiding it in the future.

☐ B) I acknowledge the mistake but focus on finding solutions together, without pointing fingers.

☐ C) I try to discuss the error indirectly, bringing up general improvement points without singling anyone out.

☐ D) I avoid mentioning the mistake to preserve the relationship but quietly work on fixing the issue myself.

When giving feedback to a team member, how much do you consider their personal feelings?

☐ A) I focus primarily on the task and how the feedback will improve performance.

☐ B) I consider their feelings but make sure the message is clear and direct.

☐ C) I carefully frame the feedback to ensure it doesn't hurt their feelings or cause discomfort.

☐ D) I avoid giving feedback directly and instead try to gently guide them toward improvement through subtle suggestions.

You're attending a business dinner in a different country. The conversation stays light, covering personal topics for most of the evening. The business aspect is only briefly mentioned toward the end. How do you feel about this interaction?

☐ A) I feel like too much time was spent on unrelated topics, and the business wasn't addressed properly.

☐ B) I understand that this is part of the culture, but I prefer more focus on the task.

☐ C) I enjoy personal interaction and see it as a valuable way to build trust for future business.

☐ D) I thrive in these environments, where relationships are built first and business comes later.

When receiving a new task or project, what kind of information do you prefer?

☐ A) I like clear, direct instructions with minimal extra context.

☐ B) I appreciate background details but prefer to focus on the main task.

☐ C) I want to understand the broader context, including why the task is important and its impact.

☐ D) I prefer to know the background and how it fits into the relationships or dynamics within the team.

A team member in a meeting seems hesitant to speak up and instead waits for others to share their opinions first. What do you think?

☐ A) They should be more assertive and contribute directly to the conversation.

☐ B) They're probably thinking carefully and will speak when they're ready.

☐ C) I understand that some people need more time to gather their thoughts before sharing.

☐ D) I think they're polite and respectful of the group's dynamic, especially if hierarchy is involved.

Scoring Guide:

Here's how to score the quiz, which has more layered options:

Mostly A's: You lean strongly toward low-context communication, valuing directness and efficiency. Task completion takes priority in your interactions, and you prefer clear, straightforward communication with minimal small talk or ambiguity.

Mostly B's: You tend toward low-context communication but appreciate the value of relationship-building. While you prefer clarity and task-focused discussions, you're also open to context and interpersonal dynamics when necessary.

Mostly C's: You lean toward high-context communication, where understanding the broader context and the feelings of others is important. You value harmony and see personal connections as a foundation for business interactions.

Mostly D's: You strongly prefer high-context communication, placing relationships and subtle cues at the heart of your interactions. You focus on maintaining harmony and navigating communication through nonverbal cues and context rather than directness.

APPENDIX D

Ice-Breaking Questions for Virtual Teams

1. What's the most unusual skill you've learned?
2. If you could have dinner with any historical figure, who would it be?
3. What's the best book you've read in the last year?
4. What's your go-to comfort food?
5. If you could instantly become an expert in something, what would it be?
6. What's the most interesting place you've ever traveled to?
7. What hobby have you always wanted to try?
8. What's a movie you can quote from start to finish?
9. If you could live in any TV show universe, which would you choose?
10. What was your first job?
11. What's the most memorable concert or live performance you've attended?
12. If you could have any superpower, what would it be?
13. What's a childhood hobby you wish you'd continued with?
14. What's the most adventurous thing you've ever eaten?

15. If you could learn any language instantly, which would you pick?
16. What's a skill you're currently trying to develop?
17. What's the best piece of advice you've ever received?
18. If you could teleport anywhere right now, where would you go?
19. What's a podcast or YouTube channel you're currently enjoying?
20. What was your favorite cartoon as a kid?
21. If you could swap lives with anyone for a day, who would it be?
22. What's a local tradition or festival in your area?
23. What's the most interesting documentary you've watched recently?
24. If you could restart your career, what would you do?
25. What's a hidden talent most people don't know about you?
26. What's the best team-building activity you've ever experienced?
27. If you could have dinner with any celebrity, who would it be?
28. What's a goal you're working towards this year?
29. What's the most unique gift you've ever received?
30. If you could instantly solve one world problem, what would it be?

References by Chapter

Introduction

The Economist Intelligence Unit. *Communication Barriers in the Modern Workplace.* The Economist Group, 2018. (Lucidchart summary PDF)

Chapter 1

Gabriel, Allison S., Daron Robertson, and Kristen Shockley. "Research: Cameras On or Off?" *Harvard Business Review*, October 26, 2021.

Grammarly and The Harris Poll. *The State of Business Communication: 2023 Report.* Grammarly Inc., 2023.

Grammarly and The Harris Poll. *The State of Business Communication: 2024 Report.* Grammarly Inc., 2024.

Hughes, Steve. "Top 10 Reasons to Keep Your Camera on in Virtual Meetings." *LinkedIn*, April 18, 2022.

McCarthy, Kimberly, Jone L. Pearce, John Morton, and Sarah Lyon. "Do You Pass It On? The Effect of Perceived Incivility on Task Performance and the Performance Evaluations of Others." *Organization Management Journal*, 2020.

Tsipursky, Gleb. "Cameras On or Off? How to Settle the Debate on Video Calls for Good." *Fast Company*, June 20, 2023.

Chapter 2

Goleman, Daniel. *Emotional Intelligence: Why It Can Matter More Than IQ*. 2nd ed. New York: Bantam Books, 1995.

Horn, Sam. *Talking on Eggshells: Soft Skills for Hard Conversations*. New York: St. Martin's Essentials, 2023.

Lencioni, Patrick. *The Five Dysfunctions of a Team*: A Leadership Fable. San Francisco: Jossey-Bass, 2002.

LeDoux, Joseph. *The Emotional Brain: The Mysterious Underpinnings of Emotional Life*. New York: Simon & Schuster, 1996.

Maister, David H., Charles H. Green, and Robert M. Galford. *The Trusted Advisor*. New York: Free Press, 2001.

Chapter 3

Deci, Edward L., and Richard M. Ryan. *Intrinsic Motivation and Self-Determination in Human Behavior*. New York: Springer, 1985.

Gallup. "Why Does Employee Engagement Research Matter?"

Herzberg, Frederick, Bernard Mausner, and Barbara Bloch Snyderman. *The Motivation to Work*. New York: John Wiley & Sons, 1959.

Maslow, Abraham H. *Motivation and Personality*. New York: Harper & Row, 1954.

Chapter 4

Ashie, Mike. "Cracking the Code: How Observing Workplace Dynamics Can Set You Up for Success." *Mike Ashie Blog*, June 7, 2023.

Hofstede, Geert. *Cultures and Organizations: Software of the Mind.* New York: McGraw-Hill, 1991.

Pollock, David C., Ruth E. Van Reken, and Michael V. Pollock. *Third Culture Kids: Growing Up Among Worlds.* 3rd ed. Boston: Nicholas Brealey Publishing, 2017.

Trompenaars, Fons, and Charles Hampden-Turner. *Riding the Waves of Culture: Understanding Diversity in Global Business.* 3rd ed. London: Nicholas Brealey Publishing, 2012.

Chapter 5

American Psychological Association. *Stress in America: Generation Z.* Washington, DC: American Psychological Association, 2018.

Castro, Hollie. "How to Help Gen Z Employees Close the Gap on Soft Skills." *Quartz*, July 13, 2023.

Clear, James. *Atomic Habits: An Easy & Proven Way to Build Good Habits & Break Bad Ones.* New York: Avery, 2018.

"Could Social Relationships Be Key to Reaching Healthy Longevity?" *National Library of Medicine*, 15, no. 12 (June 29, 2023).

Dias, John. "Gen Z Developing Fear of Phone Calls, or 'Phone Phobia'." *CBS News* New York, August 1, 2023.

Elon University. "Elon Professors Investigate the Rise of Ghosting in Job Applications." *Elon University News*, November 14, 2024.

Feldman, Ruth, Ilanit Gordon, Mor Influs, Tal Gutbir, and Richard P. Ebstein. "Parental Oxytocin and Early Caregiving Jointly Shape Children's Oxytocin Response and Social Reciprocity." *Neuropsychopharmacology* 38, no. 7 (2013): 1154–62.

Haidt, Jonathan. *The Anxious Generation: How the Great Rewiring of Childhood Is Causing an Epidemic of Mental Illness*. New York: Penguin Press, 2024.

Hersey, Paul, and Kenneth H. Blanchard. *Management of Organizational Behavior: Utilizing Human Resources*. 3rd ed. Englewood Cliffs, NJ: Prentice-Hall, 1977.

Intelligent.com. "Nearly 4 in 10 Employers Avoid Hiring Recent College Grads in Favor of Older Workers."

Little, Christopher. "A Better Way to Recognize Your Employees." *Harvard Business Review*, October 25, 2022.

Miller, Brian Cole. *Quick Team-Building Activities for Busy Managers: 50 Exercises That Get Results in Just 15 Minutes*. 2nd ed. New York: AMACOM, 2015.

McLean Hospital. "The Social Dilemma: Social Media and Your Mental Health." *McLean Hospital*, October 4, 2022.

Newstrom, John W., and Edward E. Scannell. *The Big Book of Team Building Games: Trust-Building Activities, Team Spirit Exercises, and Other Fun Things to Do*. New York: McGraw Hill, 1997.

"Research from CommBank Reveals Why Gen Z Aren't Answering Your Call." *CommBank*, June 29, 2023.

Raman, Aneesh, and Maria Flynn. "When Your Technical Skills Are Eclipsed, Your Humanity Will Matter More Than Ever." *New York Times*, February 14, 2024.

SWNS. "Gen Z Is Killing Office Small Talk—With 74% of Employees Struggling to Speak to Coworkers." *New York Post*, January 14, 2025.

Swanepoel, Annie, et al. "How Evolution Can Help Us Understand Child Development and Behaviour." *Cambridge Core*.

Visier. "Professional Ghosting: A Decision with Hidden Consequences." *Psychology Today*, April 2022.

Patel, Alok, and Stephani Plowman. "The Increasing Importance of a Best Friend at Work." *Gallup*, January 19, 2024.

Chapter 6

Carnegie, Dale. How to Win Friends and Influence People. New York: Simon & Schuster, 2009.

Ferriss, Timothy. *The 4-Hour Workweek: Escape 9–5, Live Anywhere, and Join the New Rich*. New York: Crown Publishers, 2007.

Fisher, Roger, William Ury, and Bruce Patton. *Getting to Yes: Negotiating Agreement Without Giving In*. 3rd ed. New York: Penguin Books, 2011.

Harvard Law School Program on Negotiation. "Negotiation Skills for Win-Win Negotiations." *Program on Negotiation Daily Blog*, February 11, 2025.

Sinek, Simon. *Start with Why: How Great Leaders Inspire Everyone to Take Action*. New York: Portfolio, 2009.

www.ingramcontent.com/pod-product-compliance
Lightning Source LLC
Chambersburg PA
CBHW020542030426
42337CB00013B/951